MOTORCYCLES

Life on Two Wheels

Louis Weber, CEO
Publications International, Ltd.
7373 North Cicero Avenue
Lincolnwood, Illinois 60712

Permission is never granted for commercial purposes.

Manufactured in China.

8 7 6 5 4 3 2 1

ISBN: 1-4127-1158-4

Library of Congress Control Number: 2004113591

CREDITS

Photos of 1885 Daimler (pages 8-9) courtesy of Daimler-Chrysler Corp.
Photo of 1953 Vincent Black Shadow (page 102) by Buzz Walneck.
Images of Rollie Free (page 103) and 1956 Simplex three-wheeler (page 109) courtesy of
Lake County (IL) Museum/Curt Teich Postcard Archives.
Photo of Harley-Davidson 100th Anniversary celebration (page 313)
from AP Photo/Morry Gash.
Photos of the Indianapolis Motorcycle Police Drill Team (pages 318-319)
courtesy of Lt. Jim Taylor.

Special thanks to *The Meade County Times and Black Hills Press*, local Sturgis paper since
1890, for Sturgis Rally photos (pages 60-61, 146-147, 264-265, 320).

Other photos by Doug Mitchel.

Very special thanks to the owners of the motorcycles pictured, without whose enthusiastic
cooperation this book would not have been possible.

Contents

CHAPTER ONE
1885-1919..6
The evolution from bicycles with motors to full-fledged motorcycles

CHAPTER TWO
1920-1929..28
A decade of formed fuel tanks, front brakes—and financial collapse

CHAPTER THREE
1930-1939..44
The Depression takes its ugly toll as styling takes a leading role

CHAPTER FOUR
1940-1949..64
Progress is both hindered and helped by war

CHAPTER FIVE
1950-1959..88
The "British Invasion" of music came in the 1960s. For motorcycles, it came a decade earlier.

CHAPTER SIX
1960-1969..120
What British motorcycles did in the '50s, Japanese motorcycles did in the '60s

CHAPTER SEVEN
1970-1979..176
An expansion of Japanese offerings dooms the British motorcycle industry

CHAPTER EIGHT
1980-1989..230
Market fragmentation creates a dizzying number of choices

CHAPTER NINE
1990-1999..268
British bikes return as sportbikes and cruisers gain prominence

CHAPTER TEN
The New Millennium 302
Cycles for the new century

INTRODUCTION

*I*n the early years of the twentieth century, there were literally hundreds of fledgling motorcycle manufacturers. But competition weeded out many of these enterprises, and World War I and the Great Depression killed most of the rest.

After World War II, a number of European motorcycles were added to the mix, and were joined in the late '50s by a trickle of Japanese bikes—which quickly became a flood. Soon the industry was offering specialized machines that included touring models, sportbikes, cruisers, and scramblers, giving buyers a vast array of choices.

So that the evolution of the motorcycle can be easily observed, entries in this book are arranged chronologically. The fastest bikes of their day are noted with a circular "King of Quick" label; others that are considered classics feature a "Landmark Motorcycle" plaque. Complementing these are period photos, ads, brochures, and racing shots.

Today's riders still enjoy the freedom and adventure felt by those hardy soles who made early motorcycles their transportation of choice. *Motorcycles: Life on Two Wheels* celebrates some of motorcycling's most memorable machines, and salutes the riders—both past and present—who have made this sport what it is today.

1885 – 1919

THE EVOLUTION FROM BICYCLES WITH MOTORS TO FULL-FLEDGED MOTORCYCLES

*I*n their first 35 years of existence, motorcycles went from crazy experiment to common form of transportation. Much of their appeal was economic: They typically sold for a third the cost of the cheapest cars.

By the early 1900s, numerous manufacturers had sprung up around the country. But few of these companies produced machines in any volume, and fewer still sold them nationally.

These early motorcycles were quite primitive, but the state of the art advanced quickly once demand grew. Motors gained more sophisticated intake and ignition systems, various forms of suspension were devised, drum brakes succeeded coaster brakes, transmissions and clutches were added, and kick levers replaced pedals for starting.

As technology advanced, so did sales—and so did competition. Many of the smaller companies dropped out as larger ones opened dealerships in ever-expanding markets. World War I also took its toll, and by the time the "Roaring Twenties" rolled around, only a handful of manufacturers remained.

1885 DAIMLER

Though most early motor-cycles were essentially bicycles with small proprietary motors attached, the very first motorcycle looked little like its successors. Built in 1885 by Gottlieb Daimler and Paul Maybach of Germany, it was a crude, wooden-framed contraption powered by a primitive 264-cc gasoline motor developing about ½ horsepower. A pair of "training wheels" kept the machine upright, as the rider had to sit high atop the frame on a thin leather saddle. Top speed was seven mph, about twice as fast as a normal walking pace.

WHICH WOULD YOU CHOOSE?

It's 1905. Your father owns a pharmacy, and after much begging, he has agreed to buy you one of those newfangled motorcycles for local deliveries. Only a few makes are offered in your area: the 13-cubic-inch Indian with its humpback fuel tank, the 27-cubic-inch Marsh that will probably eat more gas, or the big 32-cubic-inch Crouch with its equally big appetite. Which would you choose?

INDIAN

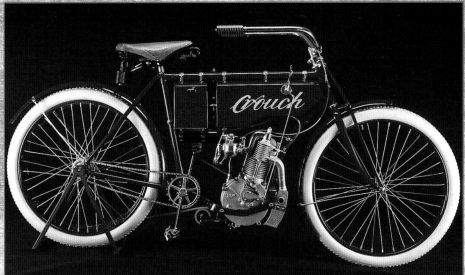

1910 PIERCE

LANDMARK
MOTORCYCLE

The innovative Pierce offered a 42-cubic-inch four-cylinder motor when most competitors had singles or V-twins. It also had shaft drive—a first for an American-made bike—along with a clutch and two-speed transmission, both rare at the time. Its massive frame doubled as the fuel and oil tanks. The Pierce was well-engineered, finely detailed, and impeccably built. But it was also very expensive, and was rumored to cost more than its retail price to build. As a result, Pierce closed its doors in 1913.

1911 EXCELSIOR SINGLE

Excelsior was part of the Schwinn bicycle empire, and in the early 1900s ranked third in sales behind Harley-Davidson and Indian. In 1911, this 500-cc single was sold alongside larger V-twins. *This page, left:* The roller beneath the drive belt adjusts the belt's tension; it is activated by the tall lever. *Above:* Intricate jointed shafts were used before the advent of cables.

1911 FLYING MERKEL

In the early days of motorcycling, Flying Merkels were the bikes to beat. Small Merkel singles of 1902 evolved into thundering V-twins by 1910, at which point the machines adopted the aptly descriptive "Flying Merkel" moniker.

The company was also known for innovation. Front forks that looked rigid were actually mounted on sliders with enclosed springs either at the top of the sliders or inside the frame neck. The design that became known as "Merkel-style forks" were popular add-ons to other manufacturers' racing bikes. Merkel was also a pioneer in rear suspension; 1910 models offered modern swingarm designs incorporating sliders similar to those used on the forks.

None of this, however, was enough to keep the Flying Merkel aloft. The 1915 models were the final offerings of one of motorcycling's most innovative pioneers.

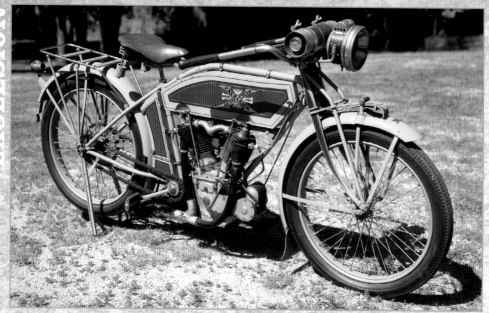

WHICH WOULD YOU CHOOSE?

By 1913, many manufacturers offered V-twin motors that were more powerful than earlier single-cylinder versions. More power meant more speed, and who wouldn't want a faster bike—especially one that was faster than the guy's down the block? Your choices include the 1000-cc Excelsior with front suspension, the similar 1180-cc Reading-Standard, or the 1000-cc Indian with front *and rear* suspension. Which would you choose?

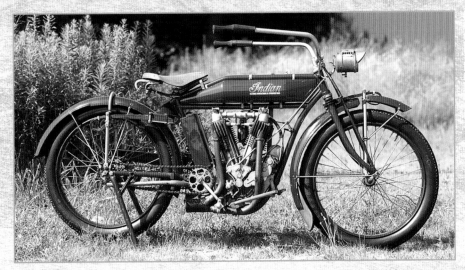

Scrapbook

By the mid Teens, motocycles had become a viable form of transportation. Larger V-twin motors allowed a passenger to be carried, and reliability was such that long trips were feasible.

For many riders, a motorcycle was their only form of transportation. That meant it had to serve rain or shine, making tire chains a useful accessory for mud or snow.

Little tykes often dreamed of the day they could have a motorcycle of their own.

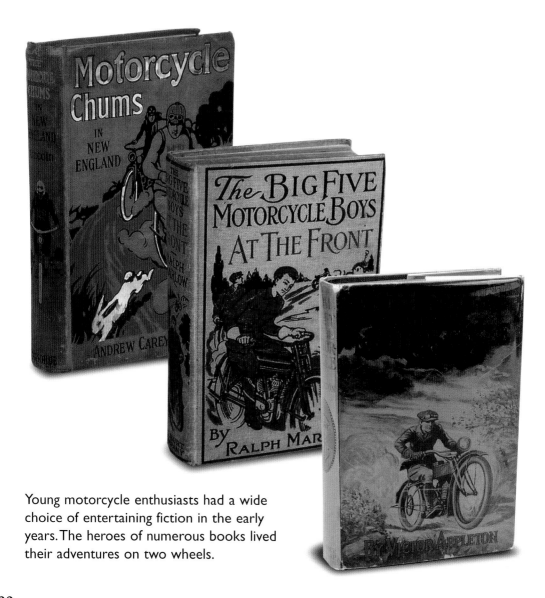

Young motorcycle enthusiasts had a wide choice of entertaining fiction in the early years. The heroes of numerous books lived their adventures on two wheels.

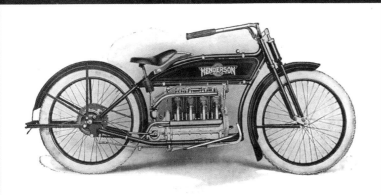

The Rider

Who wants pep in his getaway, smooth action when going slow, power in abundance for sandy hills for sidecar work, will buy a

Henderson Motorcycle Company

DETROIT

Older enthusiasts had their own form of entertaining fiction. Motorcycle ads were typically a study in hyperbole, waxing poetic over a bike's supposed virtues.

23

WHICH WOULD YOU CHOOSE?

By 1915, most motorcycles had two- or three-speed transmissions rather than a single speed, which gave them greater flexibility: low gear for quick getaways and slogging through mud, high gear for faster top speeds. Common V-twin choices included the 61-cubic-inch Harley-Davidson, the 76-cubic-inch Emblem, and the 62-cubic-inch Iver Johnson. Which would you choose?

1918 POPE L-18

Produced only from 1911-1918, Pope motorcycles were ahead of their time. The L-18 had an overhead-valve motor when most competitors used less-efficient flathead or intake-over-exhaust configurations, and a plunger-type rear suspension when most rivals had none. Contrary to that was this model's old-fashioned "gas" headlight, which used acetylene gas from a small tank to produce a flame inside the housing. By 1918, many other motorcycles had modern electric lighting systems.

1920 - 1929

A DECADE OF FORMED FUEL TANKS, FRONT BRAKES—AND FINANCIAL COLLAPSE

*B*y the 1920s, motorcycles had become a viable and accepted form of transportation. Yet due to World War I and the heat of competition, far fewer manufacturers remained in the game, the most prominent being Harley-Davidson, Indian, and Excelsior.

The pace of technology slowed during the '20s, but that isn't to say it stood still. Bicyclelike rear coaster brakes gave way to drum or external-band brakes, and front brakes—previously absent—started to appear. But the real focus during the '20s was on styling. Fuel tanks became sleeker and more prominent, as did fenders. Tires and wheels were wider and meatier, while seats were lower to the ground.

But none of this could compare to the changes that would result from the stock market crash of October 29, 1929, for the Great Depression that followed would have a profound effect on American business.

1920 Ace

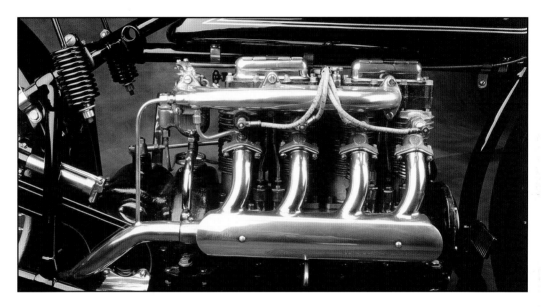

Tom and William Henderson began building four-cylinder motorcycles in 1912 but sold out to Excelsior in 1918. Two years later they were at it again, but the resulting 77-cubic-inch Ace soon ended up being purchased and marketed by Indian. In this form—and with few modifications—it continued into the 1940s, its twenty-year life span being a clear testament to its endearing design.

Scrapbook

The Shriners, founded in 1872, have long been known for establishing a number of children's hospitals—and for their motorcycle exhibitions at local events. This photo, probably taken in the mid '20s, shows the group favored Indian motorcycles at that time; in recent years, they have usually been seen on Harley-Davidsons.

RACING

During the '20s, Harley-Davidson sponsored an extremely successful racing team known as the "Wrecking Crew" for the way it demolished opponents. A stripped-down V-twin was the primary weapon of choice. As was the case with most racing bikes of the era, the only way to stop it was to hit the kill switch—or a solid object—as it had no brakes.

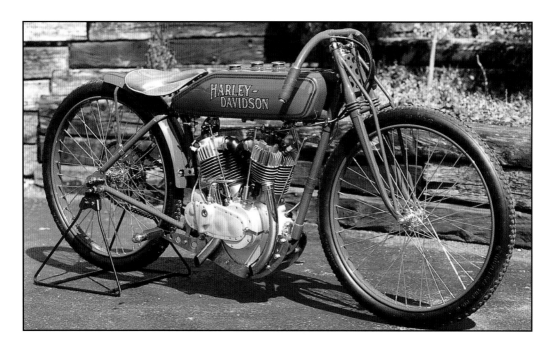

1920 Harley-Davidson 20-J

By 1920, Harley-Davidson's V-twins had adopted such "real" motorcycle features as a kick-starter (to replace pedals), three-speed transmission, and electric lights. Rear suspension, however, was still nearly 40 years away.

HARLEY-DAVIDSON

EXCELSIOR

WHICH WOULD YOU CHOOSE?

Though the number of motorcycle manufacturers had dwindled by the mid '20s, buyers of big bikes still had several choices. Harley-Davidson restyled its V-twins for 1925, giving them teardrop fuel tanks and valanced fenders; the JD featured a 74-cubic-inch motor. Excelsior's Super X was a black beauty with a 61-cubic-inch V-twin. Cleveland offered a smooth four-cylinder model, but it displaced only 36 cubic inches. Which would you choose?

1926 Brough Superior

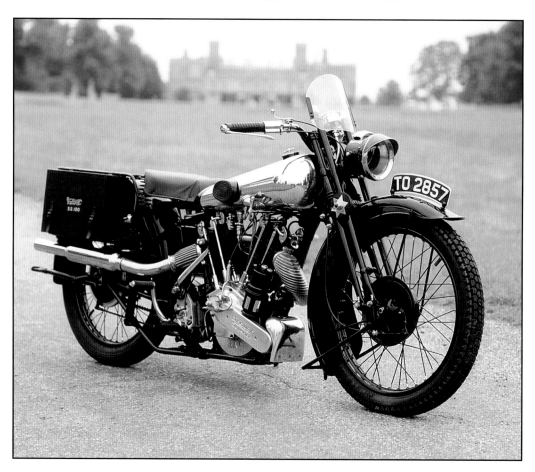

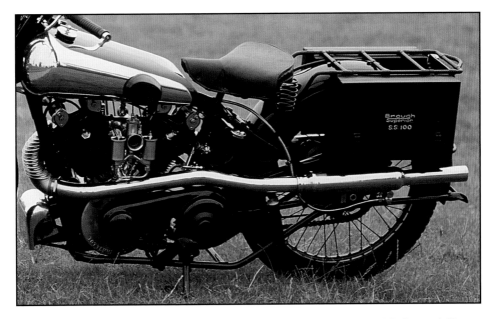

The British-built Brough Superior ("Brough" rhymes with "rough") was sometimes called "The Rolls-Royce of motorcycles." Indeed, Broughs were extraordinarily well-built machines with detail finish of a very high order. The SS 100, shown here, featured an overhead-valve 60-cubic-inch V-twin. History will always associate Brough with famed military figure and writer T.E. Lawrence, also known as Lawrence of Arabia, who was a well-known fan of the marque.

WHICH WOULD YOU CHOOSE?

By the mid 1920s, Harley-Davidson and Indian had emerged as the most prominent manufacturers, each offering a variety of models. Both lines started with a 21-cubic-inch single, popular beginner bikes for around-town errands. Indian's Prince was promoted with the slogan "You can learn to ride it in five minutes." Harley's Model BA was evidently even easier to master: Ads claimed you could "Learn to ride it in the length of a city block." Which would you choose?

Here's why it's as Comfortable as it is Dependable

1 Double acting, helical, main and buffer springs in the front fork absorb the jars and jolts of the road.

2 Low saddle position means more riding comfort and easier handling.

3 Saddle rests on cushion seat post with long spiral springs that go all the way down to the bottom of the frame.

4 Roomy footboards fitted with rubber mats—just like you see on the Harley-Davidson Big Twin.

5 Balloon tires for still more comfortable riding.

Learn to Ride it in the Length of a City Block
HARLEY-DAVIDSON
"Single"

DOWN goes your foot on the kick starter, and the motor starts. Step on the clutch. Slip the gear shift into low. Now you're riding.

Learn? Nothing to it! In the length of a city block you can learn to ride this New Harley-Davidson Single. Why, it's far easier to learn to ride than a bicycle—no pedaling. Once under way, this New Single almost keeps its own balance.

Here is a new type motorcycle that is safe and simple to operate—that is easy to ride and handle. It is low in first cost and cheap in upkeep. Think of it—80 miles and more to a gallon of gas; 800 miles to a gallon of oil; 10,000 to 12,000 miles to a set of two inexpensive tires. Forget about big garage expense—takes little more space than a bicycle!

With this new Single you can ride right up where you want to go—park it anywhere. It will take you wherever you want to go—and has all the power and speed you need. It is just the motorcycle you have often thought about and wanted—a single cylinder, easy and safe to ride, low in price, cheap in upkeep. Drop over to the Harley-Davidson dealer and see it.

HARLEY-DAVIDSON MOTOR COMPANY, MILWAUKEE, WIS.

1929 Excelsior Super X

Despite sales volumes that often trailed only those of Harley-Davidson and Indian, this 1929 Super X 61-cubic-inch V-twin was one of the last Excelsiors built. Part of the Schwinn bicycle concern, the company folded in 1931, reportedly due as much to disinterest on the part of founder Ignatz Schwinn as to financial problems brought on by the Depression. One of Excelsior's trademark styling elements lasted until the end: The forks ran through the front fenders rather than around them.

1930 - 1939

THE DEPRESSION TAKES ITS UGLY TOLL
AS STYLING TAKES A LEADING ROLE

*T*he Depression adversely affected all forms of business in the U.S., and the motorcycle industry was no exception. In fact, by 1932, only Harley-Davidson and Indian survived as major players.

With cars getting cheaper, motorcycles became a hard sell based on price alone. So a new marketing approach was tried—that of selling motorcycling as a "sport" rather than merely a means of transportation. A greater emphasis was placed on styling, flashier paint jobs appeared, and more-powerful motors were introduced. And this—along with an improving economy—kept Harley-Davidson and Indian afloat during the lean years.

1931 Harley-Davidson Model D

Harley-Davidson began switching from intake-over-exhaust to flathead V-twins in 1929. First to arrive was the new 45-cubic-inch Model D, which was intended to compete with Indian's similarly sized—and very successful—Scout. And though Harley switched its 61- and 74-cubic-inch Big Twins over to a flathead design the following year, it would be the little 45 that would make the greatest impact. It would go on to power military models in the '40s, racing bikes in the '50s, and the three-wheeled Servi-Car all the way until 1973.

1934 Harley-Davidson VLD

In 1917, Harley-Davidson adopted military Olive Green as its standard—and only—color. Initially done in support of U.S. troops in World War I, it became a tradition that was maintained for a decade after the war was over. A limited color selection was finally added in the late '20s, but it wasn't until the '30s that two-tones were available. The VLD shown opposite boasts a black and Orlando Orange paint scheme, along with an optional Buddy Seat, a two-passenger saddle introduced in 1933. Still, sidecars—as shown above—remained popular for carrying a passenger or extra cargo. This example wears Harley's Olive Green paint, still favored at the time by traditionalists.

Scrapbook

Above: A real Kodak moment, circa 1930. Though motorcycles weren't often considered four-passenger vehicles, these kids prove that where there's a will, there's a way.

Left: A mounted officer pets a friendly dog.

With her sailing cap at a jaunty tilt, this young lady
looks like a future Harley rider.

1935 Indian Chief

Despite introduction of the Ace-based four-cylinder model in 1927, the 74-cubic-inch Chief remained Indian's best-seller. The 1935 Chief received heavier, more-graceful fenders, and buyers were faced with a vast selection of options, including 13 different color choices—and an extra $5 would buy any hue DuPont offered. The Chief's long wheelbase and 480-pound heft made it a handful at low speeds, but a smooth tourer on the highway.

OVERSEAS

While the Great Depression severely thinned the ranks of motorcycle manufacturers in the U.S., European buyers of the '30s continued to face a daunting number of choices. The German-built Opel Neander was unusual for its cadmium-coated pressed-steel frame and body panels. The seat flowed into the fuel tank, almost like the sportbikes of today. The BMW R4, also from Germany, carried BMW's patented telescopic front forks, which would soon

Opel Neander

BMW R4

ODDITIES

Douglas T6

Nimbus Luxus

become almost universally used. Douglas, of England, offered a fore-aft flat twin from 1907 until World War II. Its low center of gravity made it quite successful in racing. But perhaps the oddest of the European makes was the Danish-built Nimbus Luxus. It came only in four-cylinder/shaft-drive configuration through-out its 1920-1957 production span. The flat-steel frame surrounded the fuel tank, behind which sat the centrally mounted shift lever.

1936 Harley-Davidson EL

The 1936 EL introduced Harley-Davidson's first overhead-valve V-twin, which would form the basis for all the company's Big Twins to come—and influence its future smaller twins as well. The protruding bolts on the sides of the 61-cubic-inch V-twin's valve covers prompted riders to nick-name it the "Knucklehead"—which started a certain tradition of its own.

1937 Crocker

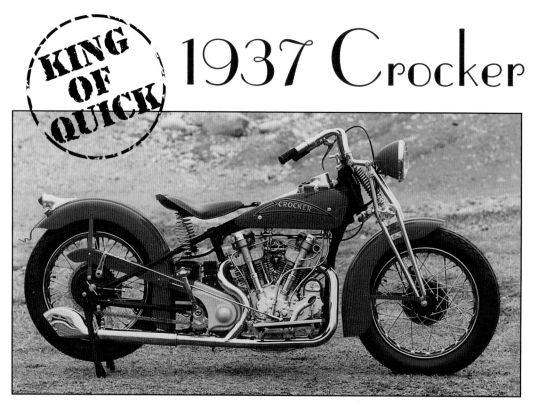

Harley-Davidson and Indian are undoubtedly the best-known American V-twins, but in terms of performance, neither could hold a candle to a Crocker. Each was built to the buyer's specifications, some with motors as large as 100 cubic inches. Two V-twins were offered, both with cast-aluminum fuel tanks: a Big Tank model and a Small Tank version. The latter, shown above, could be identified by the bolts that ran through the tank halves; opposite is a Big Tank model. Unfortunately, production was limited to only 61 examples, all made between 1936 and 1940.

Sturgis

What later evolved into the famous Sturgis Motorcycle Rally started in 1938 as a dirt-track racing event in Sturgis, South Dakota. Nine riders from four surrounding states competed for $750 in prize money. The winner was Johnnie Speiglehoff of Milwaukee (fourth from the right in white helmet) on a Harley-Davidson. The race soon evolved into a multiday event for enthusiasts, and today hosts one of the largest annual motorcycle gatherings in the country.

1938 Harley-Davidson UL

Despite the introduction—and popularity—of Harley's EL model with its 61-cubic-inch overhead-valve V-twin, the company continued to produce its flathead Big Twins: the 74-cubic-inch UL and the 80-inch ULH. Both cost less than the EL, and many buyers appreciated their ease of mainte-nance and low-speed power—perfect for hauling a sidecar. So strong was the old-timer's following that the UL continued in production until 1949.

1940-1949

PROGRESS IS BOTH HINDERED AND HELPED BY WAR

*J*ust as the U.S. was recovering from the Depression, the country entered World War II. Civilian production of many items was curtailed so factories could turn to making war materiel. Harley-Davidson—and to a lesser extent, Indian—began building military-spec motorcycles, which brought in much-needed funds. And when civilian production resumed after the war, pent-up demand brought in even more.

While postwar motorcycles were essentially warmed-over prewar versions, some technological advancements began to appear by decade's end. But so did a flood of bikes from Europe, which gave buyers a wider choice of models—and domestic makes some serious competition.

1940 Indian 440

Indian began offering four-cylinder motorcycles after acquiring the Ace Company in 1927, the first examples being little more than Aces with red paint and Indian logos. The 1940 version adopted heavily skirted fenders, and also carried a plunger-type rear suspension to join Indian's traditional leaf-spring front suspension. These motorcycles were very expensive; the list price was more than $1000, while a new Chevrolet could be purchased for less than $700.

Scrapbook

Racine County Sheriff Department
HULETT - Sheriff   1939-1940

Motorcycles have long been popular with those who keep the peace. Above: A sign at a foreign airfield gives direction and distance to several American cities. Top left: A navel commander poses with his men—and his motorcycle. Left: The Racine County Sheriff's Department show off its fleet of Harleys and Indians.

In the years after World War II, stunt riders stormed the country, setting up jumps at county fairs and local events. Here, a stunt rider leaps a dozen motorcycles in a single bound. Note the makeshift ramp—and that the rider isn't even wearing a helmet. Folks, don't try this at home.

1942 Harley-Davidson WLA

1942 Harley-Davidson XA

Opposite: The vast majority of motorcycles used by U.S. forces during World War II were Harley-Davidson WLAs. These 45-cubic-inch V-twins were based on the civilian WL model (which evolved from the Model D of the early '30s), but came specially equipped with an ammo box, machine-gun scabbard, and of course, Olive Drab paint. Roughly 80,000 were built, and many were sold as surplus after the war. These were often stripped down and fitted with aftermarket parts, fueling an early customizing trend.

Above: The XA was specially designed for desert use, with a horizontally opposed two-cylinder motor, foot-shift transmission (other Harleys were hand shift), plunger rear suspension, and shaft drive. But only 1000 were built, and none saw action overseas.

1943 Indian 741 & 841

Above and opposite, top: Like Harley-Davidson's WLA model, Indian's 741 was also used during World War II, but in far fewer numbers. Its V-twin was smaller, at just 30.50 cubic inches, and less powerful. *Opposite, bottom:* Indian also built a desert model. The 841 was very similar to Harley's XA, but it used a transverse V-twin motor instead of the XA's flat twin. Like the XA, only about a thousand were built. Unlike the XA, however, a few 841s saw military service.

1946 Indian Chief

When Indian resumed civilian production after the war, the big four-cylinder and smaller V-twin models were relegated to history, leaving only the now-legendary 74-cubic-inch V-twin Chief. As always, Indian Red was a popular color choice, though two-tones were also available. New, however, were girder-style forks adopted from Indian's 841 military model. Newly available was a spring-mounted sidecar featuring fancy chrome speedlines and trim.

WHICH WOULD YOU CHOOSE?

It's the late 1940s, and you're enticed by the idea of "wind in your hair" motoring. You don't need anything big—or expensive—so a four-stroke single sounds about right. Indian's European-styled 220-cc Arrow is a possibility, but so are a couple of new imported brands: the 500-cc BSA B33 from Britain, and the quaint Italian-built Moto Guzzi with its "flat" 500-cc cylinder and exposed "bacon slicer" flywheel. Which would you choose?

BSA

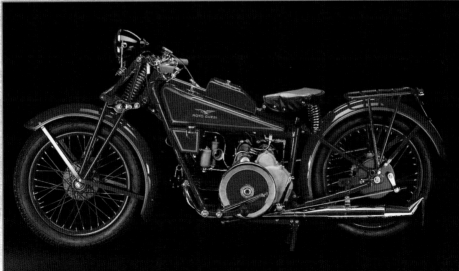

1947 Triumph Speed Twin

Introduced in 1938, Triumph's Speed Twin became the template for a whole generation of British bikes. Its 500-cc vertical-twin motor continued in production for years, eventually gaining legendary status in 650-cc form. The Speed Twin made Triumph a household name in the U.S. when importation began after World War II.

WHICH WOULD
YOU CHOOSE?

Rather than satisfy your craving for a motorcycle, the single-cylinder "starter" bike you bought merely whetted your appetite. Now you want to go big—REALLY big. In 1948, that meant the Harley-Davidson FL with its powerful overhead-valve V-twin, or the Indian Chief with its flowing fenders and flathead V-twin. Which would you choose?

INDIAN

1948 Harley-Davidson S-125

Introduced in 1948, Harley-Davidson's little S-125 put thousands of first-time riders on two wheels. Patterned after a nearly identical bike built by DKW of Germany before World War II, the S-125 had a single-cylinder two-stroke motor and foot-shift three-speed transmission. A larger 165-cc version was added in 1953, and the basic design continued to be produced into the 1960s.

1948 Harley-Davidson WL

Often called the "Forty-Five," Harley's WL evolved from the Model D of 1929. Its 45-cubic-inch flathead V-twin proved to be a durable and versatile motor, being used in the three-wheel Servi-Car *(opposite, top)* starting in 1933, the military WLA *(middle)* in the '40s, and the WR flat-track racer *(bottom)* in the '50s. When Harley's 74- and 80-cubic inch Big Twin flatheads were retired in 1949, the little 45 soldiered on. While it was finally replaced in standard motorcycles by a more modern flathead V-twin in 1951, the original design continued to power the Servi-Car until 1973.

1949 Harley-Davidson FL Hydra-Glide

The overhead-valve "Knucklehead" V-twin in Harley's big FL model was updated with hydraulic lifters and aluminum heads in 1948. Due to the revised motor's new valve covers, which looked like upside-down roasting pans, riders christened it the "Panhead." The following year, the FL gained modern telescopic Hydra-Glide forks, and Harley named the new bike after them.

1950 - 1959

The "British Invasion" of music came in the 1960s. For motorcycles, it came a decade earlier.

The suspension of civilian motorcycle production during World War II left a postwar void that took years to fill, and that pent-up demand helped open the market for imported machines from across the pond. Most were British, but other European imports trickled in as well.

At first, these small to midsize machines didn't pose a big threat to the heavyweight Harley-Davidsons and Indians. But as the 1950s dawned, it became apparent that the imports were siphoning off a good number of sales, and Indian couldn't stand the loss in revenue. Though it tried to counter with modern midsize motorcycles of its own, it was too little, too late, and Indian folded its tent in 1953. Harley-Davidson also countered—somewhat more successfully—but by decade's end, the trickle of imports had become a flood.

THE VINCENT

1951 Indian Warrior

Indian attempted to compete with the European onslaught by introducing a pair of motorcycles originally designed by Torque Manufacturing Co.—which Indian had purchased. One was the single-cylinder 220-cc Arrow, the other a 440-cc twin called the Scout. Both carried European styling and modern mechanicals, including overhead-valve motors and foot-shift transmissions, but didn't fare well against the Europeans. The Arrow was quickly dropped, while the Scout was boosted to 500 ccs and renamed Warrior. Still, sales were slow, and the Warrior died in 1952—shortly before the rest of the tribe.

1951 Whizzer Pacemaker

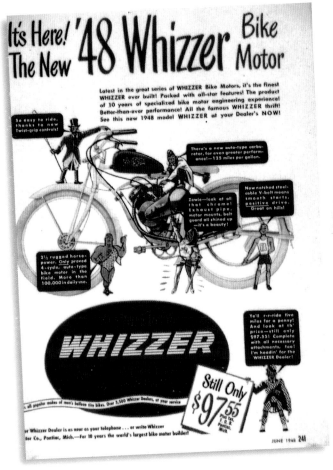

It's Here! The New '48 Whizzer Bike Motor

Latest in the great series of WHIZZER Bike Motors, it's the finest WHIZZER ever built! Packed with all-star features! The product of 10 years of specialized bike motor engineering experience! Better-than-ever performance! All the famous WHIZZER thrift! See this new 1948 model WHIZZER at your Dealer's NOW!

So easy to ride, thanks to new Twist-grip controls!

There's a new auto-type carburetor, for even greater performance!—125 miles per gallon.

Now notched steel-cable V-belt means smooth, positive drive. Great on hills!

2½ rugged horsepower. Only proved 4-cycle, auto-type bike motor in the field. More than 100,000 in daily use.

Ye'll r-r-ride five miles for a penny! And look at th' price—still only $97.55! Complete with all necessary attachments, too! I'm headin' for the WHIZZER Dealer!

WHIZZER

Still Only $97.55 Plus tax, f. o. b. Pontiac, Mich.

...all popular makes of men's balloon tire bikes. Over 3,500 Whizzer Dealers, at your service

...r Whizzer Dealer is as near as your telephone ... or write Whizzer ...tor Co., Pontiac, Mich.—For 10 years the world's largest bike motor builder!

JUNE 1948 **241**

"Hey Jack, put a *Whizzer* on it!"

Though perhaps more "motorbike" than "motorcycle," Whizzer's contribution to the sport centers more on what it did than what it was. In the 1930s, Whizzer provided a kit with a two-horsepower motor that allowed anyone with $80 and a bicycle to experience the thrill of motorized travel. After World War II, the motor was boosted to three horsepower and offered in a complete machine. These were available with all kinds of ritzy accessories and introduced thousands of riders to motorcycling. *Opposite page, lower right:* Actress Dorothy Lamour on a Whizzer.

1952 Harley-Davidson FL

A modern foot-shift/hand-clutch arrangment appeared on Harley-Davidson's Big Twins for 1952. However, the old hand-shift/foot-clutch setup was still optionally available—and would remain so until the mid '70s—as it was prefered by some riders and police departments. Also, 1952 marked the last year for the 61-cubic-inch EL model; its larger 74-cubic-inch FL sibling, introduced in 1941, was proving far more popular, and afterward stood alone as the sole Big Twin.

Never one to turn a deaf ear to its customer's wishes, Harley-Davidson continued to lavish its bikes with more chrome and polished pieces. Some additional brightwork was made standard, while accessory packages offered such niceties as chrome fender trim, chrome instrument panel, and chrome front-fender lamp.

1952 Triumph Thunderbird

LANDMARK MOTORCYCLE

Triumph's popular 500-cc Speed Twin gained a 650-cc sibling in 1950. Called the Thunderbird (years before the name was used on Ford's two-seat roadster), it was aimed at buyers who yearned for the power—but not the weight—of the big Harleys and Indians. Styling touches included a streamlined headlight nacelle and monotone paint scheme. The Thunderbird proved very popular, and earned the role of Marlon Brando's mount in the 1954 film, *The Wild One*.

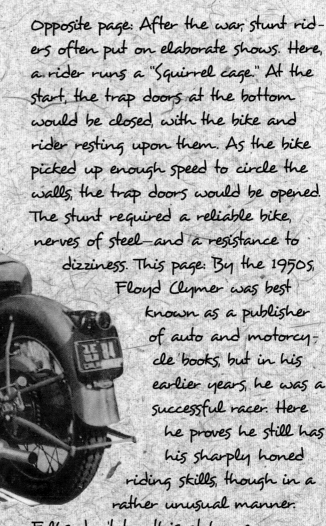

Opposite page: After the war, stunt riders often put on elaborate shows. Here, a rider runs a "Squirrel cage." At the start, the trap doors at the bottom would be closed, with the bike and rider resting upon them. As the bike picked up enough speed to circle the walls, the trap doors would be opened. The stunt required a reliable bike, nerves of steel—and a resistance to dizziness. This page: By the 1950s, Floyd Clymer was best known as a publisher of auto and motorcycle books, but in his earlier years, he was a successful racer. Here he proves he still has his sharply honed riding skills, though in a rather unusual manner. Folks, don't try this at home.

1953 Indian Chief

Though Indian had enjoyed a long and rich history, financial problems beset the company in the early 1950s. Attempts at postwar singles and vertical twins intended to compete with the machines from Europe ultimately proved unsuccessful, and their development had cost the company dearly.

By 1953, the sole surviving Indian was the V-twin Chief. Despite Indian's monetary crisis, it had been given modern telescopic forks for 1950, the same year its 74-cubic-inch V-twin was enlarged to 80 cubic inches. But the motor was still of flathead design, which by now was looking rather dated next to Harley-Davidson's overhead-valve V-twins.

According to factory records, only 600 Chiefs were built in 1953; after that, the Chief—and Indian along with it—was relegated to history. As a result, the '53 Chief is among the most collectible of Indians. It represents both the crowning achievement and the sorrowful end of a company that gave generations of motorcyclists some of their fondest memories.

1953 Vincent Black Shadow

After World War II, the British-built Vincent Rapide, with its 1000-cc V-twin, became known for its power. Then, in 1949, its faster brother appeared: the Black Shadow. Like the Rapide, the Black Shadow's motor was used as a structural frame member, and the rear suspension compressed two shock absorbers mounted beneath the seat. Though it was the fastest bike of its day, high prices killed the Black Shadow—and Vincent itself—in 1955.

Top: Depicted on this postcard is Rollie Free running a Vincent Black Shadow at Bonneville. As the story goes, after reaching 148 mph in the "normal" riding position, Free stripped down to swim trunks and swim cap and laid horizontally across the rear fender in an effort to reach 150—which he did. For this postcard, however, he was dressed in painted-on clothes and helmet.

1954 Harley-Davidson FL

Harley-Davidson celebrated its 50th anniversary in 1954 with special Golden Anniversary badges (shown in top right corner of ad) mounted on the front fenders of its motorcycles. Later anniversaries would be celebrated based on the company's 1903 founding rather than the 1904 start of production. Color-matched hand grips and kick-lever pedal were popular options, as were two-tone paint jobs and dual exhausts.

1956 Harley-Davidson KHK

When it replaced the WL in 1952, the new K-Series' V-twin maintained the 45-cubic-inch displacement and flathead design of its predecessor, but was updated and built in unit with the transmission—which now had a foot shifter. For 1954, the motor was enlarged to 55 cubic inches and the model redesignated the KH Series. A "K" suffix indicated a sport package with lower handlebars, less chrome trim, and performance-oriented cams.

Above: A 1956 ad featuring a KH depicts the entire Harley-Davidson line, from the little 125-cc Hummer to the big 1200-cc FLs. *Right:* On the May 1956 cover of Harley-Davidson's The Enthusiast magazine was none other than rock 'n' roll idol Elvis Presley astride his '56 KH.

1956 Simplex Automatic

The first U.S.-built Simplex arrived in 1935, and as the name implied, was designed with simplicity in mind. Its 125-cc two-stroke motor powered the rear wheel through a direct-drive arrangement. Later models added more features, including the automatic clutch and variable transmission used by this 1956 model.

Left: Simplex's variable transmission used a linked rubber belt and provided a range of ratios; its automatic clutch made riding in traffic easier. *Below:* Fitted with three wheels, a cargo box (similar to Harley-Davidson's larger Servi-Car), and a tow bar, the Simplex was popular with service stations, the idea being that it could be towed behind a customer's car being delivered after service work, and then ridden back to the garage.

1957 Ariel 4G Mk II

Ariel was one of the more adventurous British motorcycle manufacturers, and the unusual "Square Four" is one example of the company's bold thinking. The motor used two crankshafts—one behind the other—each driven by two cylinders, so the four cylinders were arranged in a square pattern. Upon its introduction in 1931, the motor displaced only 500 ccs; by 1936, it was up to 1000 ccs, where it remained until the model it powered—the 4G Mk II—was dropped in the late '50s. Due to their unique design, the Ariel Square Fours are now collector's items.

1957 Harley-Davidson XL Sportster

LANDMARK MOTORCYCLE

When sporting British middleweight motorcycles began attracting enthusiasts in the 1950s, Harley-Davidson responded with a sporting machine of its own. Essentially an overhead-valve version of its KH-model predecessor, the Sportster's 883-cc V-twin made it faster than its British rivals. The Sportster name would later become synonymous with performance, and continues in the Harley-Davidson lineup to this day.

1958 Cushman Pacemaker & Eagle

Cushman began building scooters in the mid '30s, and models produced during the '40s featured smooth "bathtub" bodywork enclosing the rear-mounted motor. In 1957, the Pacemaker adopted contemporary square-cut styling. Its "Step-through" design and automatic clutch made it popular in urban areas.

In 1949, Cushman introduced the Eagle which copied motorcycle styling with its "naked" motor, sprung saddle, contoured fenders, and teardrop fuel tank. Even whitewall tires were offered. A 318-cc motor and two-speed hand-shift transmission gave it a top speed of more than 50 mph.

Presenting....the excitingly new
CUSHMAN SCOOTERS
for 1959!

The Distinctive
Super Eagle and Pacemaker

For fun and excitement—as well as low-cost utility—go Cushman. Distinctive new styling for 1959 plus sturdy new construction features and new mechanical advances all mark the Cushman Super Eagle and Pacemaker as well as their companion machines, the Eagle and Road King. Famous Cushman Husky 4-cycle engine delivers up to 50 miles per hour, up to 100 miles per gallon.

Ask your dealer for a FREE demonstration ride or write for colorful booklet today. Sold and serviced nationally. Replacement parts immediately available. Dealer inquiries invited

CUSHMAN MOTORS
A subsidiary of Outboard Marine Corporation
924 No. 21st, Lincoln, Nebraska
Please send FREE Scooter booklet
NAME
ADDRESS
CITY STATE

1958 Harley-Davidson FL Duo-Glide

After more than 50 years of hardtail riding, Harley-Davidson treated Big Twin buyers to "The Glide Ride" for 1958. With a conventional swingarm suspension added to the rear, the Hydra-Glide became the Duo-Glide.

The Duo-Glide announced its newfound civility with chrome shock absorbers at the rear and chrome script on the front fender. As had long been the custom, owners often fitted their Harleys with a host of accessories; some shown here include auxiliary driving lights, turn signals, windshield, engine guard, luggage rack, saddle bags, and two-passenger Buddy Seat with grab bar. So equipped, the bikes became known as "dressers."

1959 Ariel Leader

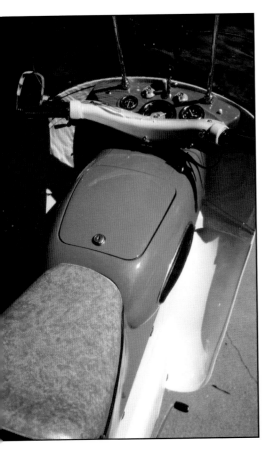

Through the 1950s, Ariel was best known for its radical 1000-cc Square Four. But a change in direction was signaled when the company dropped its big bike to bring out the equally unusual Leader. Powered by a 250-cc two-stroke motor, the Leader had a pressed-steel frame concealed by sleek bodywork. As such, it was a cross between a motorcycle and a scooter, but the combination wasn't popular with buyers, and Ariel folded in 1965.

1960 - 1969

What British motorcycles did in the '50s, Japanese motorcycles did in the '60s.

"You meet the nicest people on a Honda" proved to be one of the most successful advertising slogans of all time. Introduced in the early 1960s, it was intended to combat the negative image motorcycles—and their riders—had acquired during the '50s. It was accompanied by a new breed of smaller, "friendlier" bikes that didn't threaten any of the established makes. But other Japanese companies soon followed Honda's lead, and the motorcycles they offered became larger and more technologically advanced. Meanwhile, the American and British makes soldiered on with few changes, and by the end of the decade, found themselves outclassed and overwhelmed.

1960 Harley-Davidson FLHF Duo-Glide

Harley-Davidson still owned the big-bike market in the early '60s. Other motorcycles may have been faster, but the FLH stood unchallenged as the consummate touring bike. The 1960 version wore a sleek new headlight nacelle that would become a classic styling element still used to this day. Otherwise, the FLH carried on with its 74-cubic-inch (1200-cc) V-twin, eclipsing all competitors for sheer size and style.

1961 Velocette Venom

VELOCETTE

EUROPE'S GREATEST

British made VELOCETTE, Europe's greatest cycle—first ever to average 100 m.p.h. for 24 hours and secure a world record title, with an 'ordinary' production model too! Velocette cycles are quality designed, quality built, with quality materials. Get a "custom built" 4 stroke Velocette and join the real enthusiasts . . .

SCRAMBLER 30 cu. in.
For serious competition—up to 39 b.h.p.

▶ **THRUXTON 30 cu. in.**
A *man's* machine. Real smooth power gives vivid acceleration up to 110 m.p.h. and up to 41 b.h.p. with muffler. Up to 130 m.p.h. can be obtained without muffler.

Exclusive two-leading shoe 7½ inch front brake, well scooped for cooling, gives THRUXTON stopping power plus !

Other VELOCETTES available in 30 cu. in. class VENOM and VENOM CLUBMAN.

MAIL COUPON FOR FREE LITERATURE

MSS 30 cu. in.

A real sporty machine for the discerning rider up to 85 m.p.h. and up to 27 b.h.p.

ENDURANCE 30 cu. in.
up to 34 b.h.p.

Velocette

Equally at home on highway or range.

WEST OF MISSISSIPPI
TO: M.C. SUPPLY COMPANY, 1715 EAST FLORENCE AVENUE, LOS ANGELES 1, CALIFORNIA TEL: LUDLOW 8-2229 PLEASE MAIL VELOCETTE LITERATURE

Name

Address

EAST OF MISSISSIPPI
TO: VEHICLES LTD. INC. 18 POMFRET STREET, PROVIDENCE, RHODE ISLAND. TEL: 351-4409 PLEASE MAIL VELOCETTE LITERATURE

Name

Address

AUGUST 1966

'93

The British-built Velocette was best known for its selection of 500-cc four-stroke singles. They were high-quality machines with equally high prices, and while quite fast for a 500, they were over-shadowed by rival British 650-cc twins. Never very popular in the U.S., Velocette was one of the first British makes to succumb to the Japanese onslaught, closing its doors in 1968.

1963 Harley-Davidson FL

You're always in good company when you
Choose the Leader!

When you select *any* Harley-Davidson, you get the world's widest *choice* of models, colors, styles, accessories, clothing, and servicing products . . . all tailor-made to suit your particular riding pleasure. This exclusive combination is why Harley-Davidson continues its long-standing leadership. See your Harley-Davidson dealer. You'll be in the best of company.

Seven basic motorcycle models and the world's snappiest scooter ▲ Largest combination of models for your choice of performance, style, color ▲ Hundreds of special accessories from saddle-bags to side-mirrors ▲ Rider-tailored clothing, smartly-styled, sharpest quality, makes cycling more fun ▲ Many mechanical options . . . Customize for your own riding pleasure ▲ Friendly service . . . Wherever you ride, Harley-Davidson dealers help you feel at home ▲

HARLEY-DAVIDSON
MOTOR CO., MILWAUKEE 1, WISCONSIN

Opposite page: Aside from the windshield, this is a fairly stripped version of Harley-Davidson's big FL model. Most were fitted with saddlebags and two-passenger Buddy Seat, as shown on the red bike in the ad at left. Also shown in the ad is the full line of '63 Harleys, including *(clockwise from left)* the 175-cc two-stroke Scat, the Topper scooter, the 250-cc four-stroke Sprint, and the 883-cc V-twin Sportster.

1963 Harley-Davidson Topper

Capitalizing on the scooter craze then sweeping the country, Harley-Davidson brought out the Topper in 1960. Its 165-cc motor had a recoil starter—like a lawn mower—and drove through a variable-ratio automatic transmission.

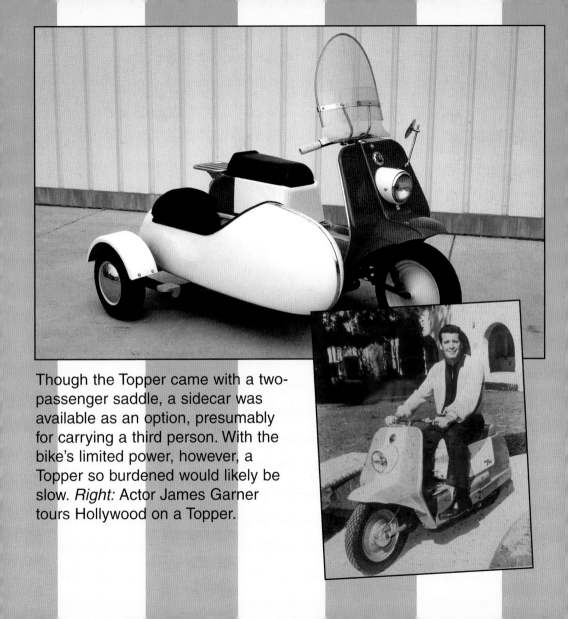

Though the Topper came with a two-passenger saddle, a sidecar was available as an option, presumably for carrying a third person. With the bike's limited power, however, a Topper so burdened would likely be slow. *Right:* Actor James Garner tours Hollywood on a Topper.

1964 Vespa Allstate Cruisaire

One of the most recognized names in scooters, Vespa is actually a model; the parent make is Piaggio of Italy. Piaggio was established in the late 1800s, eventually expanding into numerous endeavors, including aeronautics and ship-building. But the need for personal transportation in postwar Italy prompted Piaggio to "think small," and the Vespa was born. Simple and inexpensive, the Vespa nonetheless incorporated several interesting features, such as a stamped steel "frameless" chassis that enclosed a 90-cc two-stroke motor, handlebar twist-grip gear change, gear final drive, and single-sided rear swingarm and leading-link fork that allowed easy tire changes. It was an instant hit, and within ten years, more than a million were produced. In the 1960s, Sears sold a license-built copy under its Allstate brand.

1965 BMW R-27

Starting out as a builder of aircraft during World War I, *Bayerishe Motoren Werke* turned to motorcycles after hostilities ceased. Despite the change in products, the company's circular blue-and-white logo—depicting spinning propeller blades—was retained, and remains to this day.

BMW motorcycles were long synonymous with horizontally opposed twins and shaft drive, which were used on the very first examples. However, the company also produced smaller single-cylinder machines, among them the 250-cc R-27. It featured BMW's famed Earles forks, which were similar to a conventional rear swingarm in design. The featured example also has individual "swinging saddles," both of which have spring suspension.

1965 DKW
Hummel 155

DKW, *"Das Kleine Wunder"* (the little wonder) was founded in 1919 and grew to become one of Germany's most notable motorcycle manufacturers. However, it specialized in smaller bikes, none of which were exported to the U.S. in any numbers. One of those was the 50-cc Hummel 155. Upon its introduction, the European motoring press dubbed it the "Tin Banana," and indeed, it was a radical departure from any contemporary offerings. Aside from its avant-garde styling and "Darth Vader" motor cover, the Hummel was unusual in that it offered a three-speed gearbox with either hand or foot shift. In any event, it never sold well, and thus didn't last long on the market.

1965 Harley-Davidson FL Electra-Glide

Harley's big FL was treated to something new for 1965: an electric starter. No longer did Harley riders have to struggle to kick over the big 74-cubic-inch V-twin—which had a nasty habit of kicking back. Some riders shunned the idea of an "Electric leg," but it made the newly named Electra-Glide a fully modern, luxury touring bike. *Right:* Elvis Presley rode a Harley in the 1967 film *Clambake*.

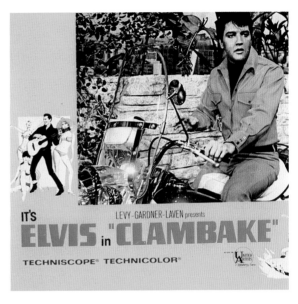

IT'S
LEVY·GARDNER·LAVEN presents
ELVIS in "CLAMBAKE"
TECHNISCOPE® TECHNICOLOR®

ROADOG

ROADOG was built by Milwaukee engineer William Gelbke in 1965. At 17 feet long and nearly 3300 pounds, it matched the length and weight of a midsize car. Its 152-cubic-inch four-cylinder automotive engine allowed it to cruise at more than 90 mph.

BLATZ

1965 Harley-Davidson Sprint

Team up with a '65 Harley-Davidson Sprint

Would you like to "quarterback" 250 c.c. of hustle? Then call your signal for a Sprint. For sheer excitement and fun — ride with your friends to high adventure. And do it aboard the hottest go-power on two wheels. You'll have the same basic engine and components that set the world's record at Bonneville.* And you'll proudly own this quality machine without paying a premium price. So join up with your buddy and test ride a Sprint now at your nearby Harley-Davidson dealer.

*Harley-Davidson Sprint "Streamliner" sets 250 c.c. World Motorcycle Speed Record at Bonneville: 156.24 mph on regular pump gas. Timed by USAC. Sanctioned by AMA.

SCAT: The ultimate in a trail machine. Really built to take it — on the road and far beyond the trail's end. Has Hi-Level exhaust and 175 c.c. engine.

(18-195)

TOPPER H: Two-wheeled excitement the entire family will take to. No shifting or clutching — has exclusive Scootaway® automatic transmission.

Manufacturer of the world's largest selection of accessories for all makes of motorcycles. Low-cost insurance easily available.

Introduced in 1961 as a result of a cooperative venture between Harley-Davidson and Aermacchi of Italy, the Sprint was powered by a 250-cc four-stroke horizontal single. Despite being quite different from other Harley products of the time, the Sprint was popular with buyers. Later versions displaced 350 ccs, but were replaced in 1974 by two-stroke machines, also built by Aermacchi.

141

1965 Marusho ST 500

Marusho was among the many Japanese motorcycle manufacturers that exported bikes to the U.S. during the 1960s. The ST 500 had a flat-twin motor patterned after that of BMW, but it was mounted in a somewhat more modern-looking machine. Despite reasonable prices—especially compared to those of its German inspiration—the Marusho wasn't very popular, and the company pulled out of the U.S. market after 1967.

1965 Triumph Bonneville

Introduced in 1959, the Bonneville was named after the Salt Flats in Utah where Triumph racing bikes had set world speed records. The "Bonny" featured a more powerful dual-carb version of the 650-cc twin used in other Triumphs, and was thus a bit faster. It was popular from the start, and though its carburetors were notorious for going out of sync with one another, the Bonneville became Triumph's most beloved model, and the name carried on through the company's end in the '80s.

LANDMARK MOTORCYCLE

146

Sturgis

During the 1960s, atten-
dance at the Sturgis Rally
grew from about 700 in
the early part of the
decade to around 2000 by
1969. Bikes of all brands
were represented; BMWs,
Hondas, and Harley-
Davidsons can be seen in
this photo.

1966 BSA Spitfire

Triumphs were better known in the U.S., but fellow British manufacturer BSA also had a devoted following. Its offerings nearly mirrored those of Triumph, but with distinct styling. The 650-cc Spitfire twin was positioned as a road racer for the street, with dual carburetors and a small two-gallon fuel tank.

149

RACING

Harley-Davidson's Sprint formed the basis for a number of successful 250- and 350-cc racing bikes in the mid 1960s—something that didn't get past Harley's advertising department. However, the bikes were Harleys in name only, as they were designed and built by Aermacchi of Italy.

151

1966 Honda 50 Super Cub

You meet the nicest people on a Honda. Like attracts like. A Honda is good-looking, personable. Always gives more than it gets. 200 miles to a gallon of gas. Upkeep minimal. And prices start about $215.* The famous four-stroke engine has a will of iron. A model of endurance. World's biggest seller. **HONDA**

FREE: Color brochure, write Dept. MJ, American Honda Motor Co., Inc., Box 50, Gardena, California 90247.   *Plus dealer's transportation and set-up charges.   © 1966 AHM

Come on in to the World of Two Wheels!

It's a world where things get done quickly. Destinations are reached just like that. Parking problems don't exist. Gas stations are seldom visited. The entry fee is low, starting about $215. And even though Honda offers the largest parts and service operation in the country—you'll rarely use it. Economy, performance and dependability—that's Honda. Where do you start? Most people usually start with a 50 or 90, and ease into two-wheeled transportation without a care. Study the various Hondas in this brochure, then ride one. Before you know it, you'll be a charter citizen of the World of Two Wheels.

It was the bike that broke Japan into the U.S. market in 1959 and went on to become the most popular two-wheeler of all time. The Honda 50 Super Cub was marketed under the slogan "You meet the nicest people on a Honda," and both the bike and slogan became world famous. With just a 50-cc motor and "step through" design it was hardly a "real" motorcycle, but the Honda 50 was soon followed by other offerings that were very real motorcycles indeed.

Honda Leads The Way...

TECHNICAL SPECIFICATIONS—HONDA CB 450

Engine type	2-cylinder, DOHC, 4-stroke
Displacement	444cc (27.17 cu. in.)
Bore and stroke	70mm/57.8mm
Compression ratio	8.5:1
Brake horsepower	43 @ 8500 rpm
Torque	27.7 ft. lbs. @ 7250 rpm
Starting system	Electric
Transmission	4-speed, constant-mesh
Suspension, front/rear	Telescopic/swing-arm
Valve clearance adjustment	External
Weight	412 lbs.

43 BHP FROM 444cc

the new Honda CB450 Here's the hot new addition to the line. A heavy-weight featuring the technical advancements and outstanding performance you expect from Honda. It's the only cycle in the country with double overhead camshafts. And torsion bar valve springs. A big bike with a big ride. If you're looking for something with more power and punch, Honda has it. The Honda CB450. See your authorized Honda dealer now. World's biggest seller. **HONDA**

SOME PEOPLE HAVE ALL THE FUN

You can easily see why. A Honda lets you go right in with suburban life. Parks anywhere. Prices start about $215.* Upkeep is next to nothing. The considerate four-stroke engine gets up to 200 mpg. And keeps quiet about it. Honda offers a wide range of models. Then there's a thing of styling. Ladies are enraptured to the store.

The Hondells

Opposite page: Honda entered the U.S. market with small motorcycles like the 50-cc Super Cub scooter and the off-road Trail 90 *(top row)*, but followed in 1966 with the potent CB450 *(bottom).* The CB450 featured electric starting and an advanced double-overhead-cam vertical twin that rivaled larger British twins for power. *This page, left:* Honda ads of the period stressed the fun factor in motorcycling. *Below:* You know you've made it when a popular quartet names their group after your bike—and puts a photo of it on their album cover.

...And Others Follow

FUN PEOPLE GO KAWASAKI

for the best of reasons!

SUPERIOR PERFORMANCE
- Plenty of low torque speed as well as high rpm power
- Oil dampened spring suspension eliminates bottoming of fork travel—the ultimate in rider comfort

BETTER STYLING
- Smart shiny appearance from every angle — yet never looks "chrome-y"
- Supersize tailight . . . largest in the industry
- Finished to the very highest standards

ADVANCED ENGINEERING DESIGN
- All engine parts are magnifluxed (x-rayed) to detect and prevent defects
- All engines have extreme heavy-duty 8 plate wet-type clutches, full circle balanced crank assembly and needle bearings upper and lower ends
- New separate forced fuel feed system (for 2-stroke models)

COMPLETE SELECTION
- A full line. Two or four stroke models. Up to a dynamic 650 cc.

SEND FOR FREE NEW KAWASAKI BROCHURE
and the name of your nearest authorized Kawasaki dealer today.

KAWASAKI

AIRCRAFT CO., LTD.
208 South LaSalle Street, Chicago, Illinois 60604
Main Office: Tokyo, Japan • West Coast Office: Los Angeles, Calif.

CYCLE/JULY 1966   17

By the mid 1960s, Kawasaki had followed Honda into the U.S. market. Like Honda, it started with smaller bikes, but by 1966 offered a 650-cc four-stroke twin— though it wasn't very popular. Ads also followed Honda's example, exclaiming that "Fun People go Kawasaki."

Yamaha also joined the fray, and with offerings similar to those of its Japanese rivals. The company stressed two-strokes until the late '60s, when it, too, introduced a 650-cc four-stroke twin—which proved very popular.

DISCOVER THE SWINGING WORLD OF

YAMAHA

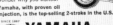

WHICH WOULD YOU CHOOSE?

HARLEY-DAVIDSON

It's the mid 1960s, and you're facing a tough choice in sporting motorcycles. Harley's Sportster ladles out loads of stump-pulling torque, but BSA's Spitfire is a lean machine with serious sporting intent, while Triumph's legendary Bonneville is the classic British twin. Which would you choose?

Customs

Early forms of customizing typically involved little more than stripping a bike of unnecessary parts and painting what was left. Famed customizer Von Dutch turned that painting process into an art form, as shown on this 1960s Triumph. Note the custom molded-in taillight.

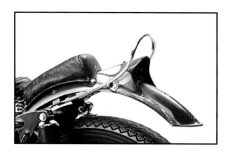

1966 Suzuki T10

Switch craft.

For more facts on the X-6 Hustler and other models write: U. S. Suzuki Motor Corp., P.O. Box 2967, Dept. P-6, Santa Fe Springs, Calif. 96070

Why is everyone switching to bewitching Suzuki?

Is it the kicky X-6 Hustler, the bike that set a world land speed record for 250cc machines at Bonneville.

Is it the Suzuki Dual-Stroke engine, the spirited master-stroke that brews up more response, more usable hp than a 4-stroke—with less urging. (Hup, two. Not Hup, two, three, four.)

Is it Posi-Force lubrication that ends oil-gas mixing for good.

Is it Suzuki's noticeably mellower pitch (so she can hear yours).

Is it the amazing comfort and safety Suzuki alone has achieved by designing for America's longer roads and riders.

Or is it the extra run—and fun—for the money the Suzuki 12 month/12,000 mile Warranty guarantees.

It's longest of the leading sportcycles and the only one with valuable trade-in provisions.

Just ask a nearby Suzuki dealer. With fifteen beguiling models, you are bound to get caught up in the spell.

solo SUZUKI

You won't be alone!

15

Suzuki began producing motorcycles in 1954, and was one of the many Japanese makes to follow Honda into the U.S. market in the '60s. By 1966, its offerings included a range of bikes topped by the T10. A 250-cc two-stroke twin, the T10 boasted a number of unusual features, including oil injection (on most two strokes of the day, the rider had to mix oil in with the gas), electric start, hydraulic rear brake, and enclosed chain, which helped keep the bike—and the rider—free from messy chain-lube splatters.

1968 Harley-Davidson XLCH

NEW RECORDS: 153.452 mph by Warner Riley in class PS-A-3000! 149.782 mph in C-A-3000!

NEW RECORDS: 141.742 mph by Robert Mauriello in class C-A-1200! 141.041 mph in PS-A-1200!

In the mid 1960s, the Sportster's 883-cc V-twin was the largest motor offered in a sporting motor-cycle, and earned the bike the nick-name "King of the Drags." A 1967 ad proclaimed the Sportster the "Fastest open bike at Bonneville," though "open" meant highly modified. Still, Harley-Davidson was probably justified in saying "Nobody builds a faster stock motorcycle"—though that claim would be short-lived. In the late '60s, the Sportster's reign would come to an end as Japanese competitors over-whelmed it with hi-tech horsepower.

1969 BMW R60

A mixture of old and new, the '69 R60 mated BMW's mid-'60s chassis and motor with new telescopic forks that replaced the traditional Earles units; the following year, BMWs got a revised flat twin and more modern chassis and styling. The R60, with its 600-cc twin, was the largest BMW offered at the time, but the revised motor would also come in a 750-cc version.

The more you know about motorcycles, the more you want a BMW.

Do you know how many different makes of motorcycles are produced in the world? More than 100. And of them all, do you know which one is best? You're right. BMW. Because since 1923, we've built our machines to one standard only—the finest that can be constructed on this earth. And that applies to every product we've turned out—automobiles as well as motorcycles.

Our list of engineering firsts is as long as your arm. Just one example

of how a BMW motorcycle is constructed: BMW uses a drive shaft instead of a chain. In fact, there isn't one chain anywhere on a BMW. Even the oil pump is driven by beautifully-finished, matched gears. No wonder BMW is the one machine so quiet, so smooth and vibration-free, you can ride it for hours without fatigue.

So how much do you know about motorcycles? It depends, friend, on whether you've ridden your first BMW. If you haven't, get on down to

your nearest dealer. When you open the throttle on that magnificent engine, when you lean into your first turn, you'll find you know all there is to know. BMW. The end.

See your nearest authorized BMW dealer, or for information write to: East: Butler & Smith, Inc., 160 W. 83rd St., New York, N.Y. 10024. West: Flanders Co., 340 S. Fair Oaks Ave., Pasadena, Calif. 91101. Canada: BMW Motorcycle Distributors, 3335 Yonge St., Toronto 12, Ontario.

Bavarian Motor Works

May, 1969

1969 BSA Rocket 3

BSA earned its reputation with four-stroke singles and twins, but in 1968 the company introduced the three-cylinder Rocket 3. Nearly a clone of the Triumph Trident, the Rocket 3's 750-cc overhead-valve motor could propel it to nearly 120 mph; later models were even faster. In 1971, a Rocket 3 was ridden to victory at the Daytona 200 race, but that would prove to be a farewell appearance; the bike was dropped shortly thereafter. *Opposite page:* The middle cylinder exhausted into two pipes, each joining with that of an outside cylinder, which then flowed into stylish "ray gun" mufflers.

1969 Honda Dream 305

After finding success with its little 50-cc Super Cub, Honda decided to bring a larger bike to the U.S. The Dream was introduced in the early '60s with an advanced, 305-cc overhead-cam four-stroke twin that seemed at odds with its dated styling and stamped-steel frame. But it could hit nearly 100 mph and be dressed with an array of useful accessories such as saddlebags, luggage rack, and windshield, all of which made it quite popular. *Above, left to right:* The chain was fully enclosed to prevent oil splatters; stamped-steel forks incorporated a leading-link suspension; the speedometer was set in a square-framed headlight housing.

1969 Honda CB 750

This is the one you knew Honda could produce. And would produce. Because only Honda had the technical skill to make it. This is the big one, Jack. The Honda 750 Four.

A four-cylinder single overhead cam engine, transversely mounted in a sleek double-cradle frame. Four carbs. And four chrome pipes— one for each cylinder—individually tuned to fever pitch. Like when you cover a standing quarter in 12.6 sec.

Honda shelled out plenty in research and development. You better believe it.

This baby was born in Grand Prix competition. And raised in the Honda heritage of power and precision. Delivers 68 hp at 8500 rpm. Hits 125 mph sans coaxing. The transmission is five speed constant mesh. An engineering marvel.

Among the new features: no fade, hydraulic front wheel disc brake. Four upswept megaphone style mufflers. Oil pressure light is housed in the tachometer. New color styles.

Your Honda dealer will have it soon. The Honda 750 Four. When you twist the throttle, remember one thing. You asked for it.

Honda 750 Four

©1969, AHM

It can safely be said that nothing in motorcycling history has ever created more of a stir than Honda's 1969 introduction of the CB750. Its four-cylinder motor was powerful and smooth, its electric starting convenient, its front disc brake reassuring, and its price nearly unbelievable. It instantly made everything else in the class obsolete.

Sooner or later, you knew Honda would do it.

Easy Rider

Peter Fonda (*below, right*) and Dennis Hopper *(left)* starred in the 1969 film *Easy Rider*, which became a runaway hit and an instant classic. Equally famous are their bikes: Both Fonda's red, white, and blue chopper and Hopper's flame-painted ride have seen numerous recreations not only by individuals, but also by companies offering custom-built machines.

1970 - 1979

An expansion of Japanese offerings dooms the British motorcycle industry

During the 1970s, Japanese manufacturers expanded their offerings into virtually every facet of the motorcycle market. Sporting middleweights attacked the British stronghold on that segment, touring models went after Harley-Davidson's traditional customers, and hi-tech, high-performance rockets started a whole new era in motorcycling. This took a fatal toll on the British makes. First to go was BSA in 1973, followed by Norton in '77, while Triumph lasted until the late '80s. Meanwhile, Harley-Davidson managed to hang on—but just barely.

The Classic British Twins

British motorcycles had gained somewhat of a cult following since being imported to the U.S. after World War II, virtually putting a stranglehold on the middleweight sporting market. Triumph and BSA were the preeminent entries, with lineups that closely paralleled each other. Both the BSA Lightning *(opposite page)* and Triumph Tiger *(this page)* were 650-cc twins, and while larger three-cylinder offerings bowed in the late '60s, twins continued to be the British mainstays.

1970 Norton Commando 750S

Norton was the third most popular British make in the U.S., but with the introduction of the Commando series in 1967, built the quickest bikes. The 750-cc Commando could keep up with the fastest machines of the day and was known for its handling prowess. The 750S model featured high-mounted exhaust, the Roadster *(opposite page)*, low-mounted exhaust.

beautiful

THE ISOLASTIC SUPER-RIDE

If you think she's just about the most beautiful thing you have seen on two wheels, then we agree.
But remember what they say about beauty being in the eye of the beholder and only skin-deep.
Mind you, when you are talking about something that has been put together with as much care and attention
as this dynamic piece of equipment, you really are talking about the ultimate.
Sleek, sophisticated, captivating, and what devastating performance figures. If you want to give her a hard time,
go ahead, she won't break up. Take this model for a ride and let yourself in for the smoothest,
most exhilarating vibration free trip you have ever had.
A precision built beauty that handles like a dream, will not let you
down and doesn't know the meaning of the word 'temperamental'.
Vital statistics: 0–60 m.p.h. in 4.8, seconds.
Standing quarter 12.6 secs. flat out performance 125 m.p.h.

The new Norton Commando Roadster

Write or call to find one of the 800 dealers—
Exclusive Importers and Distributors—East, South and
Middle West (43 States) : Berliner Motor Corp, Hasbrouck
Heights, New Jersey—07604 (201)—Atlas 8-8696.

Exclusive Importers and Distributors—West Coast (7
States) : Cal., Ariz., Nev., Wash., Ore., Hawaii and Alaska).
Norton Villiers Corp, 6765 Paramount Blvd, Long Beach,
Calif.—90805. (213) 531-7138.

Customs

The customizing trend that started in the '50s with stripped-down ex-military bikes reached new heights—and lengths—in the '70s. Special "hardtail" (no rear suspension) frames were the norm, as were radically extended forks, special fuel tanks, and custom paint jobs. Aftermarket companies supplied custom parts to make it easier for owners to create their very own "choppers."

183

SCRAMBLERS

Sometimes you feel as if you could get up and fly... so you do.

It's not just because the CT-1B Enduro 175 weighs a mere 211 pounds. It has to do with the way it's set up. This one's a dirt bike right to its soul, with a wide-ratio 5-speed gearbox to take you through the toughest terrain and Auto-lube oil injection to meter out exactly the right amount of lubrication no mat-ter how hard you're riding.

Test fly the CT-1B like the one below and on the left above. Or a slightly smaller version, the AT-1B, also shown above. Wilbur and Orville would be proud.

Yamaha International Corporation
P.O. Box 54540, Los Angeles, Calif. 90054
In Canada: Fred Deeley, Ltd., Vancouver, B.C.

YAMAHA
It's a better machine

During the '60s and '70s, off-road racing grew in popularity. Special lightweight bikes were used that had high ground clearance, lots of suspension travel, and knobby tires, but lacked lights and horns. Then came a demand for off-road bikes equipped for on-road use, and Scramblers were born. Yamaha's DT series was among the earliest and most popular, all being two-stroke singles of 125 to 400 ccs.

184

Honda's Scramblers bucked the two-stroke trend as the company was big on four-stroke motors in the '60s and '70s. In fact, its SL-350 had a four-stroke *twin*, making it heavier than most competing Scramblers, but more livable for road use. Nonetheless, Honda ads tried to push its off-road capabilities, though in reality, they weren't up to those of most rivals.

Honda Motosports eat up the dirt.

Takes a rugged bike to tame rugged country. A bike like Honda's biggest Motosport—the SL-350. Its internal-spring telescopic forks, high fender mountings and heavy-duty knobby tires turn the rough into a highway.

Dirt riding demands a powerful, dependable engine. And the Motosport 350 has the best. A famous Honda OHC four-stroke twin that whips it through the quarter in 15.3. Keeps it flying to a top speed over 80. And gives it com-

pression braking—something you can't get with the two-strokes.

The Motosport 350 has other great features, too. A tough five-speed constant-mesh transmission. Tach and speedometer. Full road lighting that's easily removed for dirt riding. And an electric starter.

The SL-350's caged at your nearby Honda dealer. Drop by and see how wild it looks. Test how well it rides. From mighty to mini, Honda has it all.

Always ride safely. Wear a helmet and observe all rules of the road. For a free color brochure, write: American Honda Motor Co., Inc., Dept. YT, Box 50, Gardena, Calif. 90247.

Motosport 350.
Eats up the dirt.

HONDA

1971 Harley-Davidson FX Super Glide

Harley-Davidson's Super Glide is often credited with being the first "factory custom." It combined the big FL model's frame and running gear with the smaller XL Sportster's slimmer forks—and threw in a boattail rear fender for good measure. The result was designated the FX Super Glide, a model name still used today.

Our featured example wears the optional Sparkling America red, white, and blue paint treatment. It's powered by Harley's "Shovelhead" V-twin, which replaced the "Panhead" in 1966. As was the case with its predecessor, the nickname referred to the shape of its valve covers and was coined by riders. Though it's a coveted collectible today, the original Super Glide didn't go over all that well. But it introduced the idea of the factory custom, which over the years has been a strong and profitable market for Harley-Davidson—and a host of other companies.

1971 Munch TTS

Embracing the philosophy that "bigger is better," Munch introduced its first bike in 1967. At a time when few motorcycles exceeded 750 ccs (Harleys excepted), the first Munch had a 1000-cc four-cylinder NSU automotive powerplant. By 1971 it was up to 1200 ccs, and had risen to 1286 by the time production wound down in the '80s. Dual headlights and a host of gauges were Munch trademarks.

WHICH WOULD YOU CHOOSE?

It's the early '70s, and you want the baddest bike on the block. A Harley Sportster would be the traditional choice, but Norton's Commando is just as fast and handles better. And then there's the smooth new four-cylinder Honda CB750, which has made a huge splash and is the obvious long-distance leader of the pack. It's a tough decision that faced thousands of buyers in the early part of the decade. Which would you choose?

HARLEY-DAVIDSON

1972 Kawasaki H2 750 Mach IV

KING OF QUICK

In the midst of a new generation of performance bikes being introduced by Triumph, BSA, and Honda, Kawasaki's 500-cc H1 Mach III two-stroke triple stood out as a ferocious performer at a cut-rate price. Introduced in 1969, it was light and very powerful, and rumors abounded of Mach IIIs that reared up and threw off their riders. But in the raging Superbike wars, "too much" was still not enough. Enter the 750-cc H2 Mach IV. It was even more fearsome than the Mach III, and for a short time at least, was the undisputed King of Quick.

1972 Triumph 650

By 1972, Triumph's venerable 650 twins were a hard sell. Ads touted their enviable racing history, but that was. . . well. . . history. In the current day, they were hopelessly outgunned by more-modern machines that often cost less. Yet Triumph's classic styling, confident handling, and strong tradition continued to attract buyers, giving the marque a welcome—if temporary—stay of execution.

Minibikes From Major Manufactures

As motorcycles grew in popularity, so did mini motorcycles—enough so that many major manufacturers offered at least one model. From a rather unexpected source came the Harley-Davidson X-90 *(below)*, with a 90-cc two-stroke motor. From Honda came a couple of four-stroke minis, including the Mini Trail 50 *(top)* and Trail 70 *(bottom)*. All are collector's items today.

1973 Harley-Davidson Servi-Car

In an incredible display of longevity, Harley-Davidson's Servi-Car was finally retired in 1973 after a 40-year run. During that time it became a favorite of police departments around the country. When introduced in 1933, the Servi-Car was powered by the same 45-cubic-inch flat-head V-twin used in Harley's Model D motorcycle. The Model D was soon renamed the WL, still with the same motor, which became known as the "45." In the early '50s, the 45 was replaced in Harley's motorcycles by a more-modern flathead V-twin, which eventually evolved into the Sportster motor with the adoption of over-head valves. But the Servi-Car soldiered on with the venerable 45 right to the end, giving this stout little V-twin one of the longest production runs of any motor ever sold in the U.S.

1973 Kawasaki Z-1

Kawasaki was already riding high on its potent two-stroke triples when it unleashed the Z-1 in 1973. Intended to beat Honda's CB750 at its own game, the Z-1's four-cylinder four-stroke motor had dual overhead cams (vs. Honda's single overhead cam), and 900 ccs of power. That the Z-1 was also great looking was just icing on the cake. It proved to be strong, smooth, and reliable, and Kawasaki found itself with a big hit on its hands.

Italian Stallions

Italian bikes have never been very popular in the U.S., but in the '70s, they led the way when it came to sporting machinery. Even conservative Moto Guzzi joined in, offering the V7 Sport with its 750-cc transverse V-twin, shaft drive, and low-set handlebars.

Ducati, long known for its sporting mounts, introduced the 750SS in 1974. It grew into the 900SS *(shown)* two years later, its powerful 900-cc V-twin and sleek fairing giving it a top speed that matched that of any Japanese rival.

MV Agusta was another Italian make known for its performance, and the 750 GT backed that up. Its 790-cc double-overhead-cam inline four was quite advanced for the day and gave the bike thrilling acceleration. But MVs were very expensive, and thus rarely seen in the U.S.

Another rare—and expensive—Italian offering was the Laverda SFC. Like Ducati's SS, it featured "cafe racer" styling with its half-fairing and fiberglass bodywork. Its 750-cc double-overhead-cam twin put out impressive power for a two-cylinder motor.

1975 BMW R90S

BMWs had amassed a reputation for quality and reliability, but were never considered "sporty." That changed with the introduction of the R90S in 1973. A 900-cc version of BMW's flat twin was joined by headlight and tail fairings, dual front-disc brakes, and a "smoked" paint job to produce a new breed of BMW that could run with the best of its Japanese and European rivals. Suddenly, BMWs were considered stodgy no more.

1975 Honda GL 1000 Gold Wing

Today. The Honda 1000.

"Honda's ultimate touring masterpiece, as the 750 Four that preceded it, will take off on a trip all its own, pioneering a sophisticated concept yet untouched but soon to be pursued by those destined to follow the leader." *Motorcyclist*, December, 1974

"The Gold Wing is completely revolutionary." *Jour de France* (France)

"...the new GL series looks to be one of the ultimates in long-distance touring machines." *Cycle World*, December, 1974

"The Honda GL-1000 is the king of motorcycles with which a man in pursuit of the best, can run a long way in a grand manner." *Car Top Magazine* (Japan)

"The four-stroke engine with specially designed exhaust system should prove to be one of the quietest motorcycles ever." *Cycle World*, December, 1974

"The bike has super-powerful disc brakes front and rear..." *Motorcycle Weekly*, October 21, 1974

"Fantastic." *MotorCycle News*, September 25, 1974 (United Kingdom)

"The new Honda GL 1000 Gold Wing, a prestigious flat-four with shaft drive, was the sensation of the world's biggest motorcycle show when it opened in Cologne..." *MotorCycle News*, September 25, 1974 (United Kingdom)

"Honda's been listening. America; although the Gold Wing will achieve international renown, it was obviously designed for the wide open spaces of the western hemisphere." *Motorcyclist*, December, 1974

"A superb example of Japanese engineering, the biggest and heaviest Honda ever made is a complete breakaway from Honda's previous designs." *MotorCycle News*, September 25, 1974 (United Kingdom)

"We can already be sure that the 1000 will be for the motorcycle world of tomorrow what the 750 Four was in 1968, the beginning of a new era." *Moto Magazine*, November, 1974 (France)

"You name it, Honda has included it in (the) Gold Wing." *Motorcyclist*, December, 1974

Never before had a manufacturer challenged Harley-Davidson's big touring machines, but the Gold Wing, introduced in 1975, hit the mark. Though other Japanese makes followed suit, the 'Wing remained the gold standard.

Early Gold Wings were usually seen wearing a fairing and travel bags, and eventually, that's the only way they were built. The smooth, water-cooled 1000-cc flat-four motor would later grow as large as 1200 ccs. 'Wings had shaft drive and an under-seat fuel tank; what looked like a fuel tank hid the electrics.

Stars On Cycles

BIG WHEELS FOR THE BIG WHEEL!

Henry Winkler starred on *Happy Days*, a top TV sitcom that aired from 1974-1984. He played Arthur Fonzarelli, aka "The Fonz," a tough-talking but lovable greaser. Here he's shown astride a modified Triumph wearing his trademark TV outfit.

Also shown favoring a Triumph is Micky Dolenz, member of The Monkees pop group, which had a TV series of its own. The group released its first album in 1966, the same year the TV show debuted.

1975 Suzuki GT 750

Suzuki went out on a limb in 1971 with the GT 750. It became known as the "Water Buffalo" due to its 750-cc water-cooled two-stroke triple—and 524-pound heft. Though not as quick as like-sized rivals, it sold well and was offered until 1977, when it was replaced by four-stroke models.

The Suzuki 750 water-cooled three.
It gets competition hot trying to keep up.

And if trying to keep up with a GT-750 is hard, you know that passing one is out of the question.

The Suzuki 750 will wind out to 120 mph.

It delivers 20% more low-end torque.

And it'll run hard all day without getting hot.

Thanks to water-cooling. Water-cooling lets the 750 run 30%

cooler than any competitive machine.

Water-cooling also gives us the closest engine tolerances we've ever made. So the 750 runs virtually noise-free. And sounds like no two-stroke you've ever heard.

Water-cooling also means the 750 won't lose any of its 67 horses due to engine heat distortion.

You can bend corners with a 750 that you've only wrinkled before. That's how good it handles.

Brakes are Gran Prix racing type: double cam, double panel. Lots of chrome

and brightwork. Outstanding paint job. Electric starter. Engine cut-off switch, CCI automatic lube.

And of course, that radiator.

Get hot, get a Suzuki GT-750.

And say goodbye to competition.

In the U.S. you can find the Suzuki dealer nearest you for free. Dial 800-631-1972.

U. S. Suzuki Motor Corp., 13767 Freeway Dr., Dept. 5023, Santa Fe Springs, CA 90670.

In Canada, Radco Sales Ltd., 1107 Homer St., Vancouver, B.C.

Member: Motorcycle Industry Council, Inc.

Suzuki: built to take on the country.

1975 Triumph Trident

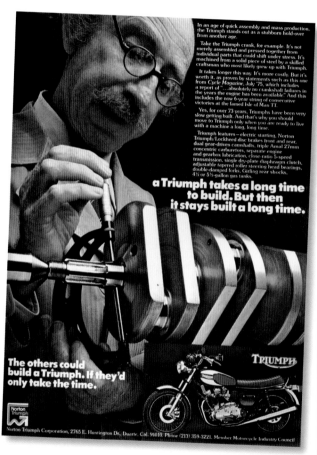

In an age of quick assembly and mass production, the Triumph stands out as a stubborn hold-over from another age.

Take the Triumph crank, for example. It's not merely assembled and pressed together from individual parts that could shift under stress. It's machined from a solid piece of steel by a skilled craftsman who most likely grew up with Triumph.

It takes longer this way. It's more costly. But it's worth it, as proven by statements such as this one from *Cycle Magazine*, July '75, which includes a report of "... absolutely no crankshaft failures in the years the engine has been available." And this includes the now 6-year string of consecutive victories at the famed Isle of Man TT.

Yes, for over 73 years, Triumphs have been very slow getting built. And that's why you should move to Triumph only when you are ready to live with a machine a long, long time.

Triumph features—electric starting, Norton Triumph/Lockheed disc brakes front and rear, dual gear-driven camshafts, triple Amal 27mm concentric carburetors, separate engine and gearbox lubrication, close-ratio 5-speed transmission, single dry-plate diaphragm clutch, adjustable tapered roller steering head bearings, double-damped forks, Girling rear shocks, 4½ or 5½-gallon gas tanks.

a Triumph takes a long time to build. But then it stays built a long time.

The others could build a Triumph. If they'd only take the time.

TRIUMPH

Norton Triumph Corporation, 2765 E. Huntington Dr., Duarte, Cal. 91010. Phone (213) 359-3221. Member Motorcycle Industry Council

Introduced alongside BSA's Rocket III in 1968, the Trident was powered by a similar 750-cc three-cylinder motor that made it among the fastest and most advanced bikes available. But what was hot in '68 was not by '69, when Honda's CB750 made every other bike of the day look dated. After a few minor updates, Triumph's triple faded from the scene after 1976.

WHICH WOULD
YOU CHOOSE?

It's the mid 1970s and there are plenty of large-displacement road burners available. But you'd prefer a bike that's lighter on its feet—and lighter on your wallet. Yamaha's sporty RD 350 uses a two-stroke twin based on a racing motor, while Honda's CB 400 has a four-stroke four that's silky smooth and revs to high heaven. Though they meet their objectives in different ways, both sporting middleweights handle curves as well as they dash down straightaways. Which would you choose?

1976 Norton Commando

By 1976, Norton's venerable Commando had been updated with a boost in displacement (from 750 ccs to 850), a switch from right-side to left-side shift (mandated by law), front and rear disc brakes, and electric start. All of this should have made the Commando more popular than ever, but it was overshadowed by Japanese bikes that offered more for less. As a result, the Commando lasted only until 1977, when it—along with Norton itself—was laid to rest.

1976 Suzuki RE-5

Following on the heels of the daring GT 750 water-cooled two-stroke came an even *more* daring bike from Suzuki: the rotary-powered RE-5. Introduced in 1975, its 500-cc water-cooled motor looked like something out of a nuclear power plant.

The 1975 version of the RE-5 featured an odd cylindrical speedometer and taillight *(below)*. But these were considered too weird on a bike that was already quite weird enough, and for '76, they were swapped for more conventional units *(opposite page)*. Still, buyers stayed away in droves, partly because the RE-5 wasn't fast but *was* expensive, and it was dropped after 1976.

1976 Triumph Bonneville

Triumph's bikes were decidedly dated by 1976, so there was little for the company to do but try to capitalize on that fact. Ads recalled Triumph's heydays of the '50s and '60s with a nostalgic look.

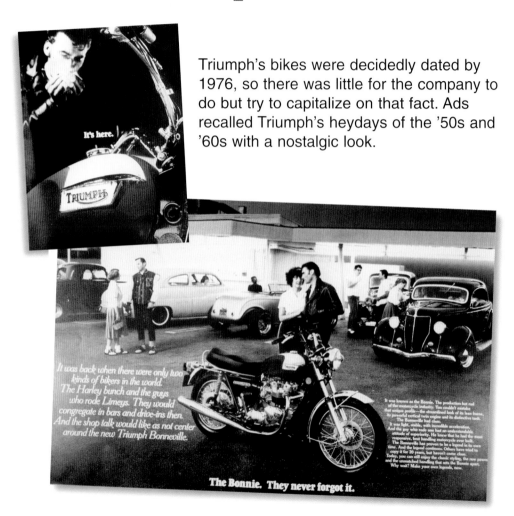

It's here.

TRIUMPH

It was back when there were only two kinds of bikers in the world. The Harley bunch and the guys who rode Limeys. They would congregate in bars and drive-ins then. And the shop talk would like as not center around the new Triumph Bonneville.

The Bonnie. They never forgot it.

Bonneville's vertical twin was boosted from 650 ccs to 750 in 1973, and by the time this '76 model was built, had gained left-side shift and front-and-rear disc brakes. Styling stayed the course—which probably worked in the Bonneville's favor—and color choices were trimmed to the blue and red shown on these pages. Despite the fact that Bonnevilles were by this time hopelessly outdated—or perhaps because of it, if the ads had the desired effect—they continued to trickle out of the factory all the way until the marque closed its doors in 1988.

1977 Harley-Davidson XLCR

ONLY ONE MAN COULD HAVE DONE THIS.

Harley-Davidson's new Cafe Racer couldn't have been built by a committee. There's no compromise.

Only one man could have built the Cafe Racer. Willie G. If he wore a suit, he'd be William G. Davidson. But he doesn't. So he's Willie G., the man who designed the Super Glide, and now, the all-new, 1977 XLCR Cafe Racer.

"I wanted to build the ultimate, no compromise bike. So I built it first, then presented it. Before the presentation, I said to myself, "If they like it, we're going to build it. If they don't, I'll keep it for myself." They liked it.

No wonder. A street legal Cafe Racer in black on black, Willie G.'s creation may be the ultimate customizing job.

He took the engine from the powerful 1977 Sportster. Sculpted the seat and rear end to resemble the famous XR-750 racer. Added a specially-designed gas tank. Put on a unique Siamese exhaust system with all black pipes.

Those pipes, coupled with the Sportster engine, make the Cafe Racer the most powerful production cycle Harley-Davidson has ever built.

Possessed with an ability to compete with the best of Europe's Cafe Racers, it can hustle down a twisting road while providing outstanding handling at high speeds.

And every detail, from the mating of aluminum cast wheels with Goodyear Eagle AT tires, to the positioning of the footpegs and the inclusion of low-profile handlebars, the careful selection of Willie G.

You'll find dual front discs matched with a single disc brake in the rear. A blunted, snub-nose, black fairing with a smoke-colored windshield. And everywhere there's black. Black trim, black cases, black horn, air cleaner cover and pipes.

Even the reproduction of the antique Harley-Davidson brass plate on the gas tank comes from the same source. "Why did I go to the old plate? I just like it."

Willie G. built himself a Cafe Racer. Now you can buy it. However, there will only be a limited number available. See your Harley-Davidson dealer for details.

Until you've been on a Harley-Davidson, you haven't been on a motorcycle.

We believe in safety first. Before you start out, light your lights, put on your helmet and watch out for the other guy. Follow owner's manual for maintenance.

In an effort to appeal to the cafe-racer crowd that favored foreign bikes in the '70s, Harley-Davidson ventured back into the world of factory customs to bring out the XLCR. Based on the 1000-cc Sportster, it featured a "bikini" fairing, angular fuel tank, solo seat with fiberglass tail section, and special "siamesed" two-into-one exhaust headers. But rivals were faster and cheaper, and the XLCR lasted only two years.

1978 Harley-Davidson FXS

Continuing the formula used for the original Super Glide of 1971, the first Low Rider featured the frame and motor from the FL-series "Big Twins" supported by the front end of the smaller XL Sportster models. The 74-cubic-inch V-twin exhaled through a two-into-one header, and a matte-black finish was used on the motor crankcase, instrument panel, and upper tank trim.

1978 Kawasaki
Z1-R/Z1-R TC

Opposite page: Kawasaki upped the Z-1's displacement to 1000 ccs, then added angular bodywork, a bikini fairing, triple disc brakes, the first factory-installed four-into-one exhaust system, and special Ice Blue paint to create the Z1-R. All of this also helped create the first stock street bike to record sub-12-second quarter-mile runs. *This page:* For those who wanted even more power, an aftermarket turbocharger kit was available. Often installed by a dealer, an example so equipped was known as a Z1-R TC, and likely prompted the factory-built turbo bikes soon to come from Honda, Suzuki, Yamaha—and Kawasaki itself.

1979 Honda CX500

While Honda may not have been as adventurous as some of its Japanese rivals during the '70s, it decided to close out the decade with a bang—or at least a loud thud. Enter the CX500, a motorcycle oddity if ever there was one. The original version *(opposite page)* was introduced in 1978. It featured a transverse V-twin like Moto Guzzi's, but the CX's was water-cooled and had four pushrod-operated valves per cylinder—an oddity in itself. It also had shaft drive, one of the first industry applications of cast wheels... and the weirdest styling of any bike on a showroom floor. A Custom edition was added later *(above)*, with somewhat more palatable cruiser styling.

1980 – 1989

Market fragmentation creates a dizzying number of choices

As Japanese manufacturers sought to broaden their product ranges, they looked to established offerings for inspiration—and tried to outdo them. Italian makes, most notably Ducati, were the infuence for sportbikes (essentially superbikes with full fairings), while Harley-Davidsons served as the template for cruisers. Add to these a host of touring bikes, motocrossers, enduros (which evolved from scramblers), along with traditionally styled machines, and the available choices became nearly limitless.

1981 Ducati Hailwood Replica

Famed racer Mike Hailwood won nine world riding
championships, many at the controls of a Ducati. So in
the early '80s, the company offered a special race
replica in his honor. Draped in the familiar red, white,
and green of the Italian flag, the replica looked very
much like a race bike. An 860-cc V-twin with Ducati's
famous desmodromic valvetrain (valves were closed
mechanically rather than by springs, eliminating valve
float), combined with a birdcage chassis and full
fairing, made it run like one as well. Behind the seat is
a fiberglass panel that can be removed, revealing a
padded perch for a passenger.

1981 Honda CBX

Honda's mighty CBX was introduced in 1978, its impressive 1047-cc twin-cam six-cylinder motor featuring an imposing waterfall of exhaust pipes. Unfortunately, performance couldn't top that of some four-cylinder rivals, so Honda repositioned the CBX as a high-speed touring bike, giving it a sleek fairing and fitted saddle bags. But that still didn't attract enough buyers, prompting Honda to drop the revolutionary CBX after 1982.

1981 Yamaha 1100 Midnight Special

During the late '70s and early '80s, Yamaha offered a line of "Specials" that ranged from midsized twins to the four-cylinder 1100. All featured the mag wheels, stepped seat, teardrop-shaped fuel tank, and high handlebars that defined "cruiser" styling. Some models added black paint, gold accents, and black-chrome headers and handlebars to become Midnight Specials. The 1100 featured shaft drive and triple disc brakes.

237

1982 Harley-Davidson FXB Sturgis

For more than half a century, the annual trek to the Black Hills of South Dakota had become a ritual for many motorcycle enthusiasts. In 1982, Harley-Davidson decided to commemorate the event with the release of the FXB Sturgis. The "B" suffix denoted "Belts," as both the primary and final drive were by toothed belt rather than chain. The Sturgis was cloaked in black with orange accents; Harley's corporate colors.

1982 Kawasaki KZ1000 R

During the 1970s, racer Eddie Lawson won numerous victories riding Kawasakis, and the company decided to build a race replica in his honor. Based on a normal KZ1000 street bike, the Eddie Lawson Replica sported a fiberglass fairing and tail piece, along with a four-into-one Kerker header—which received secondary billing on the fuel tank. The only hue offered was Kawasaki Racing Green, the company's competition color.

241

TURBOS

Turbocharged motorcycles enjoyed brief popularity during the 1980s. Typically force-fed middleweights of between 500 and 750 ccs, most couldn't match the acceleration of the biggest bikes but delivered an impressive midrange

rush. The first factory-built example was Honda's CX500 Turbo, which was based on the standard CX500 with its transverse V-twin motor. It grew to 650 ccs in 1983 *(below)*, about the same time Yamaha entered the market with its four-cylinder XJ 650 Seca Turbo *(opposite page)*. But high prices and even higher insurance rates doomed the turbos, and these hi-tech wonders faded from the scene by the end of the decade.

WHICH WOULD YOU CHOOSE?

All the Japanese companies fielded muscle-bound superbikes during the 1970s, which evolved into full-fairing sportbikes during the '80s. But in between came some transitional models with abbreviated fairings and sleek tailpieces. Among the largest were Suzuki's radical Katana 1100 *(this page)*, Honda's svelt CB1100F *(opposite top)*, and Kawasaki's race-bred KZ1000 R *(opposite bottom)*. Which would you choose?

SUZUKI

1984 BMW R65 LS

INTRODUCING THE LATEST HEIR TO 59 YEARS OF GERMAN ENGINEERING.

While the fine lines and sculpted features of most sport bikes spring from the drawing tables of stylists, those of the BMW R65LS had a different birthplace.

The drafting tables of German engineers.

As a result, they are the recipients of the same pragmatic consideration and evolutionary refinement as the legendary engine that powers this 650cc machine.

The shapely sport fairing, for example, provides much more than cosmetic appeal. It helps reduce front-wheel lift by over 30%.

The LS handlebars are low, compact, and help to provide a seating position that "is sporting in a way that Japanese bikes, even with red paint, have not discovered" (Cycle World). (High bars are also available.)

The bike's slender tail, artful as it too appears, was created in one of the most aesthetically indifferent environments known to man: the massive BMW wind tunnel in Ismaning, Germany.

Even the wheels of the LS possess a beauty that goes far deeper than their gleaming enamel. Each rim section is made of a highly rigid aluminum alloy; each hub and spoke assembly is separately cast from a far more elastic aluminum alloy to provide added flexibility. And then everything—hubs, spokes and rims—is cast as a single unit. Culminating in an exceedingly resilient "composite" wheel that not only helps increase handling prowess but decreases unsprung weight.

In the end, the BMW R65LS is one sports bike whose graceful lines do not serve as camouflage for weak engineering. For it is a machine as adept at slicing through the wind and rounding corners as it is at turning heads.

Its price? A lofty $3,790.°

But as a motorcycle columnist of AutoWeek observed, "a bad motorcycle is worthless, a good motorcycle is worth whatever it costs...By that standard, the R65LS is a bargain."

Manufacturer's suggested retail price. $3,790. Actual price will depend on dealer. Price includes state and local taxes, freight, prep, dealer prep and handling charges. © 1982 BMW of North America, Inc. The BMW trademark and logo are registered trademarks of Bayerische Motoren Werke A.G.

THE LEGENDARY MOTORCYCLES OF GERMANY.

BMW's middleweight machine, the R65 *(right)* became the sporty R65 LS with the addition of a bikini fairing, black exhaust system, two-tone paint scheme, and tail-piece with built-in grab handles. Not as quick as the sportbikes it tried to mimic, it was nonetheless a commendable sport-touring machine, which is what BMWs are all about.

1984 Honda 700S

Based on Honda's shaft-drive 650 Nighthawk introduced in 1983, the 700S that followed a year later featured a 16-inch front wheel, angular-shaped fuel tank, and bikini fairing for a sportier appearance. It was among a host of bikes from numerous manufacturers aiming to bridge the gap between "standard" bikes and full-fairing sportbikes. The 700S used a 700-cc inline four with hydraulic valve lifters along with shaft drive, both in an effort to reduce maintenance headaches.

1984 Kawasaki 750 Turbo

As a rule, the turbo bikes of the '80s weren't the fastest bikes around. But every rule has its exception, and this is it: the Kawasaki 750 Turbo. Along with its pressurized 750-cc four-cylinder motor, the Turbo was fitted with a full fairing, sculpted bodywork, and aggressive paint scheme. It still looks good today, more than

THE WORLD'S FASTEST PRODUCTI

In the great tradition of Z-1 and GPz, Kawasaki unleashes a new performance King. It's a cat-quick 750, and it's turbocharged to rip through the quarter-mile in a record-breaking 10.71 seconds. Kawasaki doesn't need huge displacement to build performance. Just the experience and heritage of dominating American drag strips for ten years. Cycle Guide Magazine, says, "That much fury contained in a 750 is almost   unbelievable." The same engineering is yours in every   Kawasaki.

Specifications subject to change without notice. Availability may be limited. Kawasaki believes in riding safely. Check local laws before you ride. Member AMA and MSF.

20 years after its introduction. Oddly, some of its closest rivals were Kawasaki's own large-displacement sportbikes, and the 750 Turbo eventually lost its crown. But it was the last and probably the best of the turbo bikes, and as such, holds a special place in motorcycle history.

1985 Kawasaki 900 Ninja

LANDMARK
MOTORCYCLE

Kawasaki's Ninja was introduced in 1984, its 900-cc four-cylinder motor incorporating a couple of Kawasaki "firsts": four valves per cylinder and liquid cooling. A sleek fairing gave it the look of a racer, and handling was impressive. Yet it was also fairly comfortable to ride, making the Ninja both a top-flight performance bike and a decent long-distance tourer. Being one of the best-looking sportbikes around didn't hurt either. The original Ninja continued to be popular well past the point when most bikes introduced at the same time were considered obsolete. It eventually lent its name to a whole range of bikes with various-sized motors, and the name carries on to this day.

1985 Yamaha V-Max

When introduced in 1985, the V-Max instantly became the undisputed King of Quick. Neither sportbike nor cruiser, the V-Max was simply a dragster for the street. Power—and a prodigious amount of it—came from a 1200-cc V-four with four valves per cylinder. The motor had a unique variable intake system that allowed great low-end torque along with 145 peak horsepower. Fast the V-Max was; subtle it wasn't. What looked like a sliver of a fuel tank was actually just a cover for the electronics, as the tank itself was under the seat. Huge aluminum scoops above the motor looked like ram-air ducts, but actually hid the horns.

Though discontinued after a couple of years, the V-Max made a comeback in the late '80s. But it was a while longer before any motorcycle managed to top its straightline acceleration.

Introducing the V-Max.

WHICH WOULD YOU CHOOSE?

It's the mid 1980s, and you want a sportbike that isn't like everyone else's. Laverda's gentlemanly RGS 1000, featuring a 1000-cc inline three, is a comfortable sport-tourer built in very low volume. Ducati's 750 F1 Montjuich, with a race-bred 750-cc V-twin and equally race-proven handling, is even more rare; only ten are being imported to the U.S. Not officially imported at all is Suzuki's RG500 Gamma, with its unique two-stroke "Square four" motor, but you've found a way to import one from Canada. Which would you choose?

LAVERDA

1987 Suzuki GSXR 750/1100

As the sportbike battle grew ever more intense, the machines themselves grew closer and closer to street-legal racers. Few bikes illustrate that point better than Suzuki's GSXR models. Introduced in 750-cc form in 1985, the GSXR750 *(opposite page)* was intended to reflect the technology learned from winning the World Endurance Championship in 1983. And differences between the race bike and the street bike were minimal. Suzuki's GSXR four-cylinder motor had four valves per cylinder and oil

cooling for better heat dissipation. Wrapped around the motor was a lightweight box-section alloy frame and full fairing, both of which further mimicked the competition version. A larger, 1100-cc version followed in 1987 *(opposite page)*. Like its kid brother, the GSXR1100 closely followed its racing heritage, and both bikes set a standard for their time.

1987 Suzuki Intruder

Japanese manufacturers began offering cruiser-style bikes in the early 1980s. Like the Harley-Davidson models they used as inspiration, most had a V-twin motor, though of smaller displacement than the big Harleys—at least at first. Suzuki's entry, the Intruder, started at 700 ccs but eventually came in much larger versions. These photos are taken from a 1987 Suzuki ad that showed Intruders with both low "dragster" handlebars and high-rise "cruiser" bars.

261

1988 Harley-Davidson
FLSTC

When introduced during the 1986 model year, the FLSTC was an instant hit. While it wasn't the first of Harley's retro-styled designs, it certainly set new standards for "Back to the Future" styling. Chief among its retro features was Harley's Softail frame, introduced in 1984, which looked like hardtail frames of old yet incorporated modern rear suspension technology. Other styling cues included old-style tank lettering, "fishtail" muffler, front and rear fender lights, and studded seat and saddle bags. Power came from Harley's Evolution V-twin, which began replacing the aging Shovelhead in 1984. The FLSTC was dubbed the Heritage Softail. It has proven so popular that a similar Heritage model remains in the line to this day.

Sturgis

By the late 1980s, the Sturgis Motorcycle Rally was drawing more than 60,000 enthusiasts each year. For the Rally's 50th anniversary in 1990, it drew an estimated 275,000. By this time, Harley-Davidsons were the most prominent make in attendence.

1988 Harley-Davidson
FXSTS Softail Springer

The FXSTS Softail Springer introduced in 1988 carried a number of classic styling elements. The springer front end, reminiscent of those used before Hydra-Glide forks were introduced in 1949, employed a leading-link design with exposed springs. In back was Harley's Softail rear end, which looked like a hardtail but wasn't. Belt drive was used, along with the 80-cubic-inch "Evo" V-twin. Shown is a Springer Softail dressed in special paint, decals, and badges to celebrate Harley-Davidson's 85th anniversary.

1990 – 1999

British bikes return as sportbikes and cruisers gain prominence

*J*ust as Phoenix rose from the ashes, British motorcycles made a comeback during the 1990s. It was a limited comeback to be sure, but heartening for enthusiasts nonetheless.

Meanwhile, the various niches—standards, sportbikes, cruisers, touring bikes, and enduros—produced some crossover models combining elements of different classes. One of the most popular was the "naked" bike, essentially a sportbike shorn of its fiberglass fairing, thus exposing its motor and exotic frame. These new models resulted in broader product lines—and more choices for consumers.

1990 BMW K1

Clad in futuristic bodywork from stem to stern, the K1 represented a stunning departure for a company that typically took a rather conservative approach with its offerings. It was aimed squarely at the sport-touring crowd, offering such amenities as concealed storage compartments in its tail section, and an antilock braking system to help provide safe stops even under less-than-ideal conditions. Power came from a fuel-injected 1000-cc flat four and flowed through BMW's traditional shaft drive that doubled as a single-sided swingarm. Bright yellow accents and graphics ensured the K1 would never be mistaken for just another BMW.

1992 Bimota Tesi

Bimota of Italy got its start in the early 1970s by wedding Honda or Kawasaki four-cylinder motors with its own exotic chassis and bodywork. Later, some Bimotas were powered by Ducati V-twin motors. Perhaps the most exotic machine to appear from this company known for innovation was the Tesi. Rather than traditional forks, the front suspension consisted of a swingarm that incorporated "hub-center steering." The handlebars acted on the lower red rod, which moved the black arm connected to the hub. The hub pivoted left and right on the axle, turning the wheel that rotated around it. While the system worked, it was expensive and offered no real advantages, making the Tesi more of a conversation piece than a huge leap forward.

1993 HARLEY-DAVIDSON FLSTN

For 1993—and *only* for '93—Harley-Davidson offered this striking black-and-white Heritage Softail with heifer trim. The company had long shown a willingness to bring daring designs to market, but this was unusual even for Harley-Davidson. Soon nicknamed the "Cow Glide," the Heritage featured retro styling cues from the '50s along with bovine trim on the seat, saddlebags, and tank top. Power came courtesy of Harley's 80-cubic-inch Evolution V-twin. Only 2700 Cow Glides were built, each with a numbered plaque beneath the tank-mounted ignition switch. Demand far exceeded supply, making them prized when new and a valuable collector's item today.

1994 Buell S2 Thunderbolt

It seemed an unlikely marriage: a lumbering Harley-Davidson V-twin squeezed into a sportbike chassis. But Eric Buell pulled it off. Buell had been building Harley-powered sportbikes since the late 1980s. Modified Sportster motors were surrounded by lightweight tube chassis and sleek bodywork to create a very unique, limited-production bike. At first, Buells didn't appeal to most sportbike buyers due to their limited speed potential. But on the street, their low- and midrange torque gave them an

advantage in normal driving. The S2 Thunderbolt of 1994 is a good example of the innovative approach to sportbikes taken by Buell. The modified 1203-cc Sportster V-twin exhausts through a huge muffler mounted beneath the motor, and the rear suspension acts on a spring located beside the muffler. Later Buells were even more innovative, with current models holding fuel in the frame and oil in the rear swingarm.

1994 DUCATI 916

Ducati specialized in savage sportbikes during the '90s, all leading up to or stemming from the 916. It represented the culmination of advanced technology and design that still seems futuristic ten years hence. In its ultimate incarnation, Ducati's traditional V-twin with desmodromic valve-train was updated with fuel injection and water cooling. Sized at 916 ccs, it spotted two cylinders and nearly 100 ccs to most competitors. Yet combined with a lightweight chassis boasting sensational handling, it managed to power the 916 to numerous victories on racetracks around the world. Successors to the 916 displaced up to 998 ccs, but all looked nearly identical to their forebearer. And each is highly prized by anyone lucky enough to have wrapped their hands around the throttle.

STURGIS

The annual celebration in Sturgis, South Dakota, seems to get bigger every year. Motorcyclists from around the world pack into the small town and surrounding areas the first week of every August. Whether it's a happy couple on a Harley, Santa spreading good cheer on his three-wheeled "sleigh," or "Junky Jim's" rat bike loaded down with souvenirs, colorful bikes—and bikers—can always be found.

1996 Boss Hoss

No doubt about it, this is the biggest, baddest motorcycle on the street. And lest it be discounted as some kind of one-off absurdity, rest assured the Boss Hoss is a production vehicle—though production is admittedly limited. Powering this ultimate expression of the "bigger is better" philosophy is a Chevrolet V-8. Most examples, such as the one pictured, use a 350-cubic-inch version—that's 5700 ccs—but newer models are available with a 502-cubic-inch motor. Horsepower output ranges from 355 for the base model to a whopping 502 for the hottest version. A Boss Hoss appears huge, and its looks are not deceiving. The lightest of these motorcycles tips the scales at 1100 pounds (a full-dress Harley weighs about 850). They're also expensive; figure about $30,000—to start.

Customs

Many customs of the 1990s adopted a low, "stretched" look, forsaking the long, raked forks of their predecessors. Motors were typically built by after-market manufacturers such as S&S, and though they *looked* like Harley-Davidson V-twins, they were usually larger and more powerful. Paint jobs were often monochromatic, in contrast to the wild designs used in the '70s.

1997 DUCATI
750 MONSTER

While a swoopy, full-coverage fairing was a defining necessity for any self-respecting sportbike of the '90s, a new breed of performance machine was beginning to bloom. Stripped of all nonessentials, bikes like Ducati's Monster were starting a new trend toward minimalist motorcycles. On the Monster, there was nothing to shroud the tubular steel frame or V-twin motor. As opposed to Ducati's race-inspired sportbikes that carried exotic four-valve, water-cooled V-twins, the Monster came with a simpler air-cooled, two-valve motor. As a result, the Monster followed a formula that proved so successful with American muscle cars of the '60s: light weight, powerful motor, basic amenities, all combined with a low price. Introduced in 1993 with a 900-cc V-twin, smaller 750- and 600-cc Monsters followed.

1997 Harley-Davidson Fat Boy

For 1990, Harley-Davidson released what would become one of its most popular models. Though the Fat Boy carried retro styling cues used by some of its siblings, it had a unique front-fender design and was the only bike in the line to feature solid wheels front and rear. The original 1990 version came only in grey, and that color has never been offered again; as a result, the '90 is somewhat of a collector's item. Fat Boys have otherwise received only minor changes since, and still retain the distinctive "winged" tank logo of the original.

1997 TRIUMPH

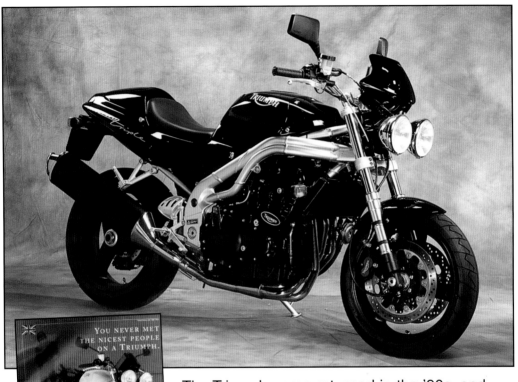

The Triumph name returned in the '90s, and though the bikes had nothing to do with their predecessors, some models carried names from the past. One was the Daytona sportbike *(opposite, top)*, another was the Thunderbird *(opposite, bottom)*. A "naked" bike with bug-eyed headlights *(above)* got a new name: T509.

All three were powered by a three-cylinder motor; it displaced 885 ccs in the T509 and Thunderbird, 955 in the Daytona. Other models offered four-cylinder motors of up to 1200 ccs.

RACING

Above: Sportbike racing became more and more popular during the '90s as the competing bikes became closer and closer to their street-going counterparts.
Left: These aren't your father's sidecar rigs. In fact, sidecar racers bear a closer resemblance to go-karts than to motorcycles. While never very popular in the U.S., sidecar racing is exciting to watch.

Motorcycle racing takes many forms, and some don't require warm weather. Ice racing is popular in many parts of the world, and the action is much like that of dirt-track racing, with riders sliding and fishtailing around turns. The bikes themselves also resemble dirt-track racers—except for the studs on their tires.

1997 Ural

If the Russian-built Ural looks remarkably similar to a BMW, that's only because it is. After World War II, Russia seized BMW's plant in Germany and moved the tooling and equipment back to the Soviet Union. There they built what were essentially reproduction BMW motorcycles with Ural badges. Today's models are little-changed. The 650-cc horizontally opposed twin still uses overhead valves, and sidecar versions retain the option of having a powered wheel that comes in handy on rough terrain. In front is a modified Earles fork similar to those used on pre-'69 BMWs. Though it looks ungainly today, a Ural with sidecar cost just $6000 in 1997, a transportation bargain. And the fact that the 60-year-old design is still in production is also an off-hand compliment to its original German maker.

1998 HARLEY-DAVIDSON BIG TWINS

Since 1957, Harley-Davidson's V-twin lineup had always been divided between Sportsters, with a smaller-displacement motor built in-unit with the transmission, and Big Twins with larger displacement and separate motor and transmission. By 1997, Big Twins came in many different forms. Among the most popular was the Road King *(opposite page, top)*, introduced in 1994, which carried '60s retro styling along with touring amenities such as saddle bags and windshield. The Heritage Springer *(opposite page, bottom)*, often known as the "Old Boy," looked even further to the past with '40s styling, including a springer front end and fender-mounted running light. More modern was the Wide Glide *(below)*, which sported cruiser styling and got its name from its widely spaced fork tubes. All those shown are dressed in special paint schemes offered only in 1998 to celebrate Harley-Davidson's 95th anniversary.

1998 HONDA VALKYRIE

Cruisers had traditionally been powered by V-twin motors, but Honda broke the established mold with the Valkyrie. Hung from its frame was the massive, chrome-encrusted 1500-cc flat-six motor from the company's Gold Wing touring bike. In power and smoothness, the Valkyrie set a new standard for the cruiser class, one that has yet to be challenged.

DAYTONA

Held on the Florida shore every March since 1942, Daytona Bike Week draws thousands of riders on all types of bikes from across the U.S. Among the activities is the annual running of the Daytona 200 motorcycle race. *Below:* Like the similar event in Sturgis, South Dakota, colorful characters abound; this rider, evidently not content with the amount of heat buildup in his helmet, decided to give it a fur coat—and horns.

The New Millennium
Cycles for the New Century

*A*s motorcycling entered the twenty-first century, the popularity of the sport was on the rise. So were the number of model choices, as old makes reappeared and new ones emerged.

Becoming a larger part of the scene were factory-built choppers offered by numerous independent companies. In many ways these "backyard builders" mimicked those that started the motorcycle craze more than a century before. Some offer a line of models, others custom-build each bike to the customer's specifications, but nearly all are powered by proprietary V-twin motors.

In the end, it doesn't really matter what kind of bike is chosen; it's the excitement of the ride that counts. And if the current level of enthusiasm is any indication, the sport of motorcycling will be going strong well into the *next* century.

2000 Harley-Davidson FXSTD

Harley-Davidson took custom styling a step further in 2000 with the FXSTD Deuce. A stretched fuel tank and straight-cut rear fender were its strongest visual cues; less obvious were the unique "turbine blade" solid rear wheel, gracefully tapered fork legs, and teardrop headlight. Power came from a new generation of V-twins called the Twin Cam 88. Introduced in 1999, it replaced the beloved Evolution motor that dated from 1984.

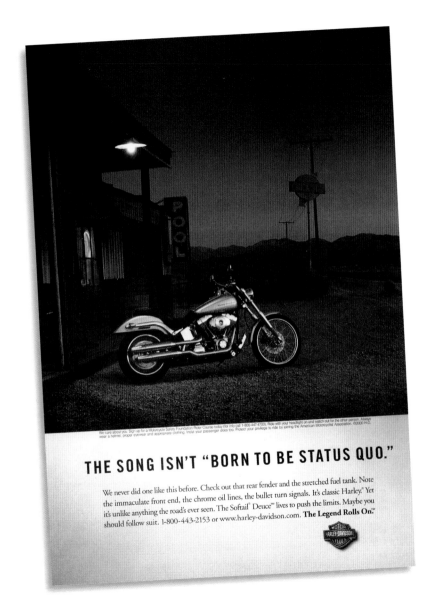

THE SONG ISN'T "BORN TO BE STATUS QUO."

We never did one like this before. Check out that rear fender and the stretched fuel tank. Note the immaculate front end, the chrome oil lines, the bullet turn signals. It's classic Harley.® Yet it's unlike anything the road's ever seen. The Softail® Deuce™ lives to push the limits. Maybe you should follow suit. 1-800-443-2153 or www.harley-davidson.com. **The Legend Rolls On.**™

2000 MV Agusta F4 Strada

Twenty years after the last production model rolled off the assembly line, MV Agusta made a comeback. Or at least the name did. Purchased in 1991 by Cagiva (which also owned Ducati at the time), the MV name was eventually placed on a limited-edition, $32,000 sportbike called the F4 Oro. Made of exotic, lightweight materials, the Oro was replaced by a slightly less-exotic F4 Strada that looked nearly the same, but sold for "only" $19,000. With that, sales took off, and MV was back.

2000 Suzuki Hayabusa

Introduced in 1999 with a highly tuned 1300-cc water-cooled four-cylinder motor, Suzuki's "Busa" raised the sportbike performance bar with sub-10-second quarter-miles and a top speed in excess of 180 mph— *well* in excess, according to some. Hyabusas came with a humpbacked bubble covering the passenger seat that was intended to aid aerodynamics, but gave an awkward look to a bike that wasn't praised for its appearance in the first place. As a result, many riders leave it off. Aerodynamics drove the design of the Hyabusa, as it plays an important role in top speed when the speeds being considered are this high. Suzuki reportedly spent hours in the wind tunnel refining the shape, because the Hyabusa was intended to be the quickest, fastest bike around. Which it turned out to be. And still is.

KING OF QUICK

Customs

As custom creations become wilder, it takes some creative thinking to make one stand out—which is the whole idea in the first place. And these creations stand out indeed. *Opposite page:* It's unlikely another quite like this will ever be seen. Note the speckle-painted frame, twin-tube swingarm, and rear disc brake carrying triple four-piston calipers. *Above:* Its license plate reads "DRMSCL" (Dreamsicle), and the paint scheme reflects the colors of the popular frozen treat. Almost everything not painted is chromed.

Harley-Davidson's 100th Anniversary

Harley-Davidson celebrated its 100th anniversary with a big party in its hometown of Milwaukee—and with special badges on its bikes. *Below:* An estimated 150,000 people crowded into Milwaukee's Veterans Park on August 31, 2003, to celebrate Harley's first 100 years; they represented only a fraction of the total number of visitors to the city during the four-day event.

RACING

Competitors in the American Motorcyclist Association (AMA) Superbike class ride essentially stock street machines. *Above:* A Kawasaki Ninja displays impressive lean angle. *Opposite page:* A Suzuki GSXR leads a Honda RC-51 through a fast corner.

2004 Victory

NEVER HEAR,
"YOU HAVE THE SAME BIKE I DO."

VICTORY CUSTOM ORDER PROGRAM · AUGUST 1 – OCTOBER 22, 2004

DREAM IT. BUILD IT. ORDER IT. Any Victory,® including the all-new Victory Hammer,™ built exactly the way you want it. Custom paint. Wheels. Saddlebags. Engine and frame color. Chrome packages. Touring packages. Many options you can't get anywhere else. You dream it. We build it. And since it's built at the factory, it comes with the quality, warranty and savings to match. Start designing your custom Victory now at VICTORYMOTORCYCLES.COM

THE NEW AMERICAN MOTORCYCLE™

In the mid 1990s, the demand for Harley-Davidsons far exceeded supply, buyers often waiting two years for delivery. That prompted three new U.S. Motorcycle manufacturers to try and cash in on the shortfall. The Excelsior name from the '20s was brought back to grace a V-twin cruiser that was introduced with high hopes, but sold poorly and was soon dropped. The revered Indian name was also resurrected—for the umpteenth time—for another V-twin cruiser, and that attempt lasted longer, but also ultimately failed. More successful was the Victory, a division of the same company that builds Polaris snowmobiles and ATVs. Initially offered in a cruiser style like the others *(1997 model shown below)*, recent versions *(opposite page)* took on more of a custom look.

Scrapbook

Founded in 1954, the Indianapolis Police Motorcycle Drill Team is made up of full-time police officers performing on the same motorcycles used for patrol duty.

The group has performed at numerous events around the country, including Presidential inaugural parades, Harley-Davidson rallies, and The Orange Bowl football game.